A TASTE OF GOA

MRIDULA BALJEKAR

A TASTE OF
GOA

MRIDULA BALJEKAR

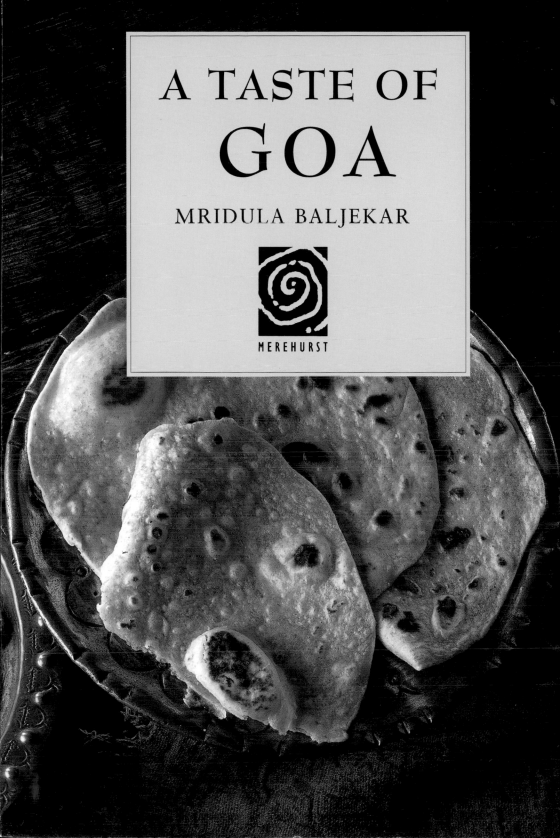

MEREHURST

Published in 1995 by Merehurst Ltd
Ferry House, 51-57 Lacy Road, Putney London SW15 1PR

Copyright © Mridula Baljekar
ISBN 1 85391 469X

A catalogue record for this book is available from the British Library.
The right of Mridula Baljekar to be identified as the Author of this
Work has been asserted by her in accordance with the Copyright,
Designs and Patents Act 1988

Edited by **Val Barrett**
Designed by **Sara Kidd**
Photography by **Alan Marsh**
Styling by **Rebecca Gillies**
Food for Photography by **Jo Craig**

Colour separation by Global Colour, Malaysia
Printed by Craftprint, Singapore

Previous pages: Mung Bean Usal, Mutton Curry and Chapatties.

This book is dedicated to my father-in-law,
Ramdas Narayan Baljekar,
who was born in Goa
on 1st September 1914.

AUTHOR'S ACKNOWLEDGEMENT

My thanks to Major J. M. Esperanca Da Silva and his wife Louisa who were in England at the Staff College, Royal Military Academy, Sandhurst, for their help in elaborating on some of the Portuguese names and cooking techniques.

My deep indebtedness to two books, Jill Norman's "Complete Book of Spices" and Tom Stobart's "Herbs, Spices and Flavourings" which have been invaluable in compiling the Glossary.

My thanks also to two noted chefs of India, Cyrus Todiwala and Thomas Braganza of the Taj Group of Hotels in Goa. They and their Staff discussed various dishes with me and directed me to many small cafés and restaurants in my search for authentic Goan recipes.

Many loving thanks to my family for the support and enthusiasm they showed during the time of writing this book.

Last, but not least, I am grateful to my father-in-law, for diligently proof-reading each and every recipe!

CONTENTS

INTRODUCTION

The Land:

Lush green hills, 1,000 metres high, gently descending to the coastal plains; a vast patch-work of paddy fields, their raised borders lined with swaying palm trees; a network of nine rivers criss-crossing the landscape and bringing fertile silt; long sandy beaches and the deep blue Arabian Sea; Christian churches, Muslim mosques, Hindu temples; rennaisance and baroque, terra-cotta and brick; tall-masted fishing boats and long meandering roads. This is Goa, where nature has conspired to slow down the rat race to a stroll; where one day stretches languidly into the next.

Today, in spite of the trespass of technology, Goa seems suspended between ancient and modern and its basically unspoilt character lives on.

Goa drips with history and heritage. The county grew around the port of Goa, which controlled the spice trade with the East. Arabian merchants bought silks, spices and precious stones, travelled to Venice and sold them on at astronomic prices to the Europeans. Western seamen soon realised the benefit of cutting out the middle man and, in the early 16th century, embarked on their quest to colonise India. In 1510 the Portuguese landed on the west coast of India, and subsequently created an Eastern Empire for themselves, with Goa as the capital.

With their new found wealth the Portuguese developed a resplendent and impressive county with magnificient architectural achievements. This grandeur is evident even today in the beautiful cathedrals, churches and mansions. Gold, mined in Africa, was used to coat the altars of Goa's churches giving it the name 'Goa Dourada' or Golden Goa. Portugal had annexed Goa at the height of its own imperial power, and very soon Goa came to be known as 'The Pearl of the East'.

The decline of Portugal's stature in Europe, and the opening of a new port in Bombay, contributed to the dilution of Portuguese power in the colony. Their rule in Goa lasted four and a half centuries and owed some of its success to their attempts to create a degree of harmony between the three predominant religions i.e. Hindu, Christian and Muslim. In December 1961, fourteen years after the rest of India had gained its Independance from British Rule, the Portuguese finally departed. They left behind a land which, within a short space of time, became the focal point of the world's tourists.

Goa today is a kaleidoscope of cultures, but through it all still seeps the delicate essence of age old Indian conservatism in day-to-day life.

The Religions:

The Hindus had ruled this part of India for about 1,500 years. Towards the end of the fifteenth century the Muslims gained the upper hand until they, in turn, were defeated by the Portuguese. Early attempts to convert the local population to Christianity had its problems: temples were demolished, mosques were razed to the ground.

The arrival of the Jesuit Father, Francis Xavier, in 1542, calmed a volatile situation and there evolved a degree of tolerance between the religions. It is a tradition which, especially in the villages, has not faded with the passing of time.

Today, the people belonging to all three religions not only respect each others customs and rituals, but actively participate in the fun and enjoyment. Festivals of the three religions are celebrated in style by the whole community. The famous Festival of Goa is celebrated before the period of Lent. It is a blend of Portuguese and Latin American influences and is the only one of its kind in India; at the same time 'Holi', the Hindu festival of splendid colour, is celebrated to mark the onset of Spring.

The birth of St.Francis Xavier, the Patron saint of Goa, is remembered on December 3rd. After his death his body refused to decay and is now kept in a glass casket in the famous church, The Basilica of Bom Jesus. Towards the end of November, 'Id-e-Milad', the birthday of the Muslim prophet Mohammed, is celebrated amid much delight. As the year draws to a close, Goa wears a festive look for the Christian festival of Christmas.

Tourism:
The sublime natural beauty with rivers and streams, hilly tracts and lush green valleys, rice fields, coconut palms and clusters of cashew trees, together with miles and miles of golden beaches, make Goa a perfect tourist spot. The hotels here have a strong European flavour. Some of the major luxury hotels are typical examples of Portuguese villages.

The bullfight is another Portuguese legacy as well as the cleanliness of the streets and the self-discipline of the people. All this makes a tremendous impact on the tourist and it is quite easy to forget that one is, in fact, in India!

Tourism is a major industry in Goa and the season lasts from the middle of November to early January. The sea is warm, the landscape green from the recent monsoons and there is an abundance of most tropical fruits.

The Food:
Eating Goan food can be a unique experience. Indian cuisine is well known for its regional variations; but Goa, being only a small part of the country, offers an amazing variety within the state itself. Three main religions, Hindu, Muslim and Christian, influenced Goan cuisine and gave it that unique touch. Then there is the most prominent influence of the Portuguese, who were in Goa for nearly four centuries. All of this has given Goan cooking its own distinct style and flavour.

I found it a totally delightful experience to cook and taste the recipes and my family and friends shared that delight with me. I have no doubt you will thoroughly enjoy the results of your efforts and that will be the most rewarding aspect for me!

Bon Appetit!

Easy Route to Confident Goan Cooking

Cooking Utensils:

No special utensils are needed for successful Goan cooking, but it is important to make sure that your pots and pans have tight-fitting lids and a heavy base. A heavy-based pan is essential to ensure even cooking. Lids that fit well stop the liquid from evaporating quickly thereby enabling you to produce the required quantity of sauce. A tight-fitting lid is even more crucial when cooking rice.

Electrical Gadgets:

A food processor, a blender and a coffee grinder are very useful in preparing ingredients. In Goa, spices are traditionally ground on a grinding stone. Fine powders and pastes are the key to smooth sauces. A blender or a food processor will do this job beautifully. Use your food processor to chop, slice and purée onions. Fitted with an appropriate blade, you can also make dough for all Goan bread in your processor.

A coffee mill is very effective in grinding dry spices, though it involves grinding in batches. Desiccated coconut, especially, needs grinding in several batches. The texture of desiccated coconut is not fine enough to produce a smooth sauce. This is the reason why you need to grind it in the coffee mill first. You can get a very fine desiccated coconut from most Indian stores, sold as 'Coconut flour'. This is ideal and does not involve pre-grinding. If you intend to grind a lot of spices yourself, it is a good idea to keep a coffee mill solely for this purpose or you may sometimes have strangely flavoured coffee!

Preparing Garlic and Ginger:

The two items you will need most are garlic and ginger. If these are kept ready, Goan cooking will seem infinitely easier and quicker. I have them ready to use in the fridge and store a large quantity in the freezer.

Peel and chop fresh ginger and purée in the food processor without adding any water. Store a small quantity, in an airtight container, in the fridge if it is going to be used within a few days. Here, it will last for 2-3 weeks, though it will change to a light brownish colour; this will not affect the flavour or colour of your dish. Divide the remaining quantity into smaller portions and store in the freezer in suitable freezer containers.

Similarly, peel garlic and prepare and store as for ginger. Follow the guidelines below to judge quantities required for the recipes:

Fresh root ginger:	Purée
1-2.5cm ($^1/_2$ -1 inch) cube	$^3/_4$ -1$^1/_2$ level teaspoons
3.5-5cm (1$^1/_2$ -2 inch) cube	2$^1/_4$ -3 level teaspoons
5cm (2 inch) cube	3 level teaspoons

Fresh cloves of garlic:	Purée:
2-4 large	$1^{1}/_{4}$-$2^{1}/_{2}$ level teaspoons
6-8 large	$3^{3}/_{4}$-5 level teaspoons
10 large	$6^{1}/_{4}$ level teaspoons
2-4 small	$^{1}/_{2}$-1 level teaspoon
6-8 small	$1^{1}/_{2}$-2 level teaspoons
10 small	$2^{1}/_{2}$ level teaspoons

Storing unprepared fresh root ginger:

Ginger should never be stored in the fridge: it will soon start going mouldy, as ginger hates moisture! Store it in a cool dry place, preferably in an earthenware pot. The best company for ginger are potatoes; store it together with potatoes in a cool dry place away from direct light.

Storing unprepared fresh garlic:

Treat it exactly the same way as ginger. This way they will last infinitely longer than in the fridge.

Storing fresh green chillies:

Fresh chillies will last much longer if the stalks are removed. As soon as you bring them home, wash them and remove the stalks. Dry thoroughly on absorbent paper. You can store a small quantity for immediate use in the fridge in a plastic food bag; these will last 10-15 days. For long term use, put them in a freezer bag and store in the freezer. As they can be used straight from the freezer, you can freeze all your stock. The seeds inside will discolour when you thaw them; but if you are going to remove the seeds this will not matter. When a recipe calls for whole fresh chillies, put them in straight from the freezer; this way the seeds will retain the original colour.

Storing fresh coriander:

If you buy a big bunch of fresh coriander, as sold by Indian grocery shops and other greengrocers, first clean them by removing all the roots. Next remove all the yellow/brown/black leaves. Wash and prepare the required quantity for your recipe and wash the rest thoroughly. Chop them in the food processor or with a sharp knife and put in suitable freezer container. Freeze until required. Prepared this way, coriander will be perfect when it is required to be stirred into the sauce or ground with other ingredients. For garnishing, you should use only the fresh leaves as they look so pretty. They can be cleaned as above and stored in the fridge, wrapped in foil, for up to 10 days.

Freezing cooked Goan dishes:

Recipes which are suitable for freezing are indicated as such. Do make sure you cool the dishes quickly and thoroughly. Put them in suitable freezer containers with appropriate labels and chill before finally putting them in the freezer. Provided you have used all fresh ingredients to start with, you can safely freeze the dishes for 6-8 months.

Thawing and re-heating:

Always thaw slowly in the fridge. Re-heat gently on top of the stove, adding a little water as and when necessary, so that the sauce does not dry out and returns to its original consistency. Please do not panic if your thawed dish looks watery! This is because some separation will take place during the thawing process; when you start re-heating, the meat or poultry or vegetables will re-absorb the water. You can re-heat most Goan dishes in the microwave; rice re-heats beautifully this way. Bread, pies, pakode etc. will not re-heat successfully in the microwave. The grill, or the oven, is best for these.

What to drink with your Goan meal

Goan's enjoy drinking. Unlike the rest of India, home grown wine accompanies most Goan meals. Goan wine is said to be one of the best in India and it tends to be rather dry. If you like dry white wine, a well chilled glass will go down well with your meal. Medium dry white wine also complements Goan food. Beer and lager are popular too, but my favourite is a glass of chilled, strong dry cider and plenty of chilled plain water with ice and lemon!

The most popular drink in Goa is 'Feni' of which there are two varieties. They are both made of the coconut palm and the cashew fruit. These are enjoyed as an aperitif, with meals when mixed with other mixers and as after-dinner tipples. Cashew Feni is also referred to as the poor man's brandy!

Glossary

Asafoetida (Hing): A dried, resinous gum obtained from several species of a tropical plant similar to the garden fennel. It is sold ground as well as in solid pieces, and is used in very small quantities when cooking vegetables, beans and lentils and making pickles. It has a strong flavour on its own, but when combined and fried with other spices, this strong, slightly unpleasant flavour disappears.

Atta or Chapatti Flour: 'Atta' is a very fine wholemeal flour used to make all Indian unleavened bread. The whole wheat kernel is ground very fine to give us a product which is rich in dietary fibre. 'Atta' is sold under the brand name 'Chapatti Flour' and is available in all Indian grocery stores.

Bay Leaf (Tej Patta): Bay leaves used in Indian cooking are obtained from the cassia tree and are quite different from Western bay leaves, which come from the sweet bay laurel. As the Indian variety are rarely available in the West, standard bay leaves may be used

Caraway Seeds (Shahjeera or Royal Cummin): Caraway is related to the parsley family and the seeds look like cummin though they are much smaller.

Cardamom (Elaichi): There are two main varieties, the small green type (Choti Elaichi) and the big dark brown type (Badi Elaichi). There is also a third variety which is white; these are simply blanched green cardamoms. Green cardamoms have a mellow flavour and are used in whole or ground form in sweet and savoury dishes. The brown ones have a coarse skin and a more pungent flavour.

Cassia and Cinnamon: Cassia comes from the dried bark of the tropical plant of the same name. Cinnamon is obtained from the dried bark of a tropical plant related to the laurel family. True cinnamon comes in quill form and cassia, though it starts as a quill, is sold in pieces because it breaks quite easily. Although they produce similar flavours, cassia is more pungent. They are used for flavouring sauces in whole or ground form and used whole to flavour Pullaos and Biryanis.

Chillies (Mirchi): Chillies vary tremendously in shape, size and pungency. It is very difficult to judge the strength of a chilli but, as a general guide, large fleshy ones tend to be milder than the small, thin-skinned ones. The hottest part of a chilli is the seed. To achieve a mild flavour, always remove the seeds.

Fresh green chillies (Hari Mirchi): The long slim variety, used all over India, are available from Indian grocery stores and some local greengrocers. Mexican chillies such as Jalapeno and Serrano are more commonly available in supermarkets; although these are not ideal for Indian cooking, they can be used when a recipe calls for fresh chillies to be chopped or ground with other ingredients to make chutneys and spice pastes.

Dried red chillies (Lal Mirchi): When fresh green chillies are left on the plant until they are ripe, they change to a rich red colour. These are then dried to obtain dried red chillies, the flavour of which totally changes during the drying process. The small, pointed

Following pages: A vibrant array of herbs, spices and fresh ingredients essential to Goan cuisine.

ones, known as 'Bird's Eye' chillies are very hot and are used whole in small quantities to flavour oil. Long, slim ones are less pungent and are used ground with other spices. Dried red chillies are ground to a fine powder to make chilli powder.

Clarified Butter (Ghee): Ghee has a rich and distinctive flavour and can be heated to the same temperature as oil. Ghee can be stored at room temperature indefinitely. You must take care, however, not to use wet spoons.

Cloves (Lavang): Unopened, dried buds of an ever-green tree grown extensively in Southern Asia, they have a strong, distinctive flavour and should be used in small quantities. They are used both whole and ground, and it is best to grind cloves at home in small quantities using a coffee mill.

Coriander, fresh (Hara Dhania): The fresh leaves of the coriander plant are used for flavouring as well as garnishing Indian dishes. The fruit produced by the mature coriander plant is the seed which is used as a spice.

Coriander, seed (Dhania): One of the most important ingredients in Indian cooking, coriander has a sweet, mellow flavour. It blends extremely well with chicken and fish.

Coconut, fresh (Nariyal): Coconut palm grows in abundance in Southern India and Goan cuisine thrives on the use of this versatile fruit. The flesh is grated and ground with spices and the milk is extracted from the grated coconut to make rich sauces. In the West, four convenient alternatives are available: Desiccated Coconut, Creamed Coconut, Coconut Milk Powder, and Canned Coconut Milk. These are easy to use and they produce excellent results.

Coconut Toddy: This is the sap that is extracted from the coconut palm tree to make vinegar in Goa. Goan housewives use roof tiles to make coconut vinegar at home. The coconut sap is filtered and stored in a covered ceramic jar for a few days. The tiles are heated until they are red hot and dropped into the Toddy to start the action of bacteria which sours the Toddy in 3-4 weeks. The result is an excellent, mild and fruity vinegar which is ready to use in 3-4 weeks.

Cider Vinegar: Cider vinegar is an excellent substitute for traditional Goan vinegar. It adds a lovely fruity flavour to the dish.

Curry Leaf (Kari Patta): These have a rather assertive flavour and they grow wild in Southern India and the foothills of the Himalayas. The dried leaves are sometimes used in making curry powder.

Fennel Seeds (Saunf): These have a taste similar to Anise. The seeds are bigger than cummin and are greenish-yellow.

Fenugreek (Methi): This is a very strong and aromatic herb and both the seeds and the leaves are used in cooking. The fresh leaves are lightly spiced and cooked as a vegetable. The dried leaves, known as Kasuri Methi, are used to flavour vegetable and some meat dishes. The seeds, which are tiny and creamy in colour, are used in minute quantities to flavour the oil before cooking lentils and vegetables.

Garam Masala: The word 'garam' means heat and 'masala' is blending of different spices which can be cooked or raw. It is commonly used in Indian cooking, though in

Goa individual spices are roasted and combined to produce different flavours. The main ingredients are cinnamon, cardamom, cloves and black pepper to which other spices, according to preference, can be added.

Ginger (Adrak): Fresh root ginger gives an authentic hot flavour with a warm woody aroma. Dried, powdered ginger cannot be used as a substitute.

Mustard (Sarsoon or Rai): There are three types of mustard seed. Black and brown mustard seeds are commonly used in Indian cooking and are interchangeable. White mustard seeds are used in Northern India for making pickles. Black and brown seeds are fried in hot oil to lend a nutty flavour to a dish. The seeds are also combined with other spices and ground to make special spice pastes. The green leaves are used as a vegetable.

Nutmeg (Jaiphal): Nutmeg comes from a plant which is very unique as it produces two fruits in one; nutmeg and mace (Javitri). Nutmeg has a hard dark brown shell with a lacy covering which is mace. Both nutmeg and mace are used sparingly as they have a highly aromatic taste. Pre-ground nutmeg does not have as much flavour as freshly ground, as it loses its flavour quite quickly. Special nutmeg graters, with a compartment to store a whole nutmeg, are available in kitchen equipment shops or departments.

Paprika: Paprika is made from the dried and powdered flesh of a mild sweet variety of pepper found in Hungary and Spain. Indian paprika, however, comes from a special type of mild chilli pepper known as 'Deghi Mirchi', grown in Kashmir. It lends a brilliant red colour without making a dish hot.

Poppy seeds (Khus Khus): White poppy seeds are used in Indian cooking and are obtainable from Indian grocery shops. The seeds are either ground as they are, or roasted and ground to add a nutty flavour as well as to thicken and enrich the sauce. Black poppy seeds are not used in Indian cooking.

Rose water: There is a special strain of rose which is cultivated solely for culinary purposes. The petals are used to garnish rich Mogul dishes and the essence is extracted for use in sweet dishes. The essence is diluted to make rose water which is used for both sweet and savoury dishes.

Sesame Seeds (Til): These are a pale creamy colour. and are used whole for making sweets and ground for flavouring vegetables and thickening sauces. They have a lovely, rich and nutty flavour. Black sesame seeds are not used in Indian cooking.

Tamarind (Imli): Tamarind grows extensively in India; the tender pods are green, resembling a pea pod, but longer and thicker. When the fruit is ripe, the colour changes to a rich dark brown and the tender outer skin turns to a hard shell. Dark brown, sticky tamarind flesh encases the seeds which have to be removed. The flesh is soaked in hot water before making a pulp which adds a distinctive tangy flavour to a wide range of Indian dishes. Ready-to-use concentrated tamarind pulp offers a very convenient alternative.

Turmeric (Haldi): Turmeric is related to the ginger plant. The fresh rhizomes are similar in appearence to fresh root ginger. These are dried and ground before being sold commercially. Turmeric adds a rich golden colour and a light aroma with a fresh flavour.

SOUPS, STARTERS AND FINGER FOODS

Caldo Verde
SERVES 4-6

A simple and delicious soup containing puréed potato and spinach. A good stock is the key to the success of this soup. You can buy good stock from supermarkets these days, but please avoid stock cubes. The recipe below makes a wonderfully aromatic stock which you can use for other soups and stews in this book.

For the stock:
2.5 litres (4 pints) water
1 cooked chicken carcass, 250g (8oz) approx. cut up
250g (8 oz) raw beef bones
250g (8 oz) raw lamb bones
250g (8 oz) onions, un-peeled and quartered
4 large cloves of garlic, un-peeled and lightly crushed
5-6 slices of fresh root ginger, un-peeled and sliced
1 teaspoon black peppercorns
125g (4 oz) carrots, un-peeled and thickly sliced

For the soup:
15g (½ oz) butter
1 medium onion, approx. 180g (6 oz), finely chopped
4 cloves of garlic, peeled and crushed
2.5 cm (1 inch) cube of fresh root ginger, peeled and grated
600ml (1 pint) stock
250g (8 oz) boiled potatoes, finely chopped
125g (4 oz) fresh spinach, finely chopped
½ teaspoon salt or to taste
½ teaspoon freshly milled black pepper
150ml (5 fl oz) single cream

Preparation time: 10 minutes if stock is made in advance
Cooking time: 15 minutes

To make the stock:
1. Put all the ingredients for the stock in a saucepan and bring to the boil. When the liquid begins to boil, skim off scum from the surface. Cover the pan and simmer for 45-50 minutes.
2. Leave the saucepan in a cool place and when the contents are completely cold, place it in the refrigerator for 2-3 hours.
3. After this time, the fat will solidify. Remove the solid fat with a perforated spoon or spatula and strain the stock.
4. This stock can be stored in the refrigerator for at least one month provided that you boil it every 3-4 days. You can, of course, freeze the stock in required quantities and use as necessary.

To make the soup:
1. Melt the butter and fry the onion, garlic and ginger gently until the onions are soft, but not brown.
2. Add the stock, potatoes, spinach and salt. Bring to the boil, cover the pan and simmer for 10-12 minutes. Remove from heat, allow to cool slightly.
3. Purée the soup in a blender or food processor.
4. Return the soup to the saucepan. Add pepper and cream and heat until very hot but not boiling.

Suitable for freezing.

Previous pages: Stuffed Crab and Caldo Verde.

Stuffed Crab
SERVES 4

The influence of European culture on Goa's heritage is reflected in its cuisine. Here one sees the perfect marriage of Eastern ingredients with Western cooking styles.

4 cooked crabs weighing approximately 500g (1 lb) each

3 tablespoons sunflower oil

1 small onion, approx. 125g (4 oz), finely chopped

1-2 fresh green chillies, seeded and finely chopped

2 teaspoons peeled and grated fresh root ginger

2 teaspoons peeled and grated or crushed garlic

3 teaspoons ground coriander

60g (2 oz) red pepper, seeded and cut into 0.5cm (¼ inch) cubes

125g (4 oz) shelled and cooked fresh or frozen peas

½ teaspoon salt or to taste

125g (4 oz) fresh tomatoes, skinned and chopped or canned chopped tomatoes, drained

15g (½ oz) chopped fresh coriander leaves

2 tablespoons lime juice

Preparation time : 30 minutes
Cooking time : 15 minutes

1. Lay the crab on its back and break off the claws and legs with a twisting action. Tap claws and legs gently with a rolling pin to crack them without breaking into lots of small pieces. Extract the meat and discard the shells.

2. Pull the centre portion from the main shell. Extract the meat with a teaspoon. Use a skewer for the stubborn bits. Discard the thick dark brown bits. Discard the stomach sac, gills and lungs. Wash the shells and wipe dry with absorbent kitchen paper. Brush lightly with a little sunflower oil.

3. Preheat the oven to 190C, 375F, Gas Mark 5. Heat the oil over a medium heat and fry the onions and green chillies until the onions are soft but not brown. Add the ginger and garlic and fry gently for 1 minute.

4. Add the ground coriander, red pepper, peas and salt. Cook for 2 minutes, stirring constantly. Add the tomatoes. Stir and cook for 2 minutes.

5. Stir in the crabmeat, fresh coriander and lime juice. Mix well and remove from the heat.

6. Put the spiced crabmeat into the shells.

7. Line a baking sheet with foil and place the stuffed crab shells on it. Bake in the centre of the oven for 15 minutes.

Serve with lettuce, slices of tomato and cucumber and wedges of lime.

Suitable for freezing. Freeze stuffing on its own, without shells.

Tomato and Coconut Soup
SERVES 4

*T*his soup is based on a lovely tomato and coconut broth known as 'Tomato Saar' from the 'Saraswat' range of recipes. The word 'Saar' means an extract which is flavoured with a few simple spices and enriched with coconut milk. It is rather watery and is used to moisten the rice or as a drink with meals. I have, however, adapted the recipe to make it suitable to serve as a soup. It is important that the soup is not allowed to boil, as coconut will curdle at high temperatures.

2 tablespoons sunflower oil
$^1/_2$ teaspoon black mustard
  seeds
1 tablespoon curry leaves
Pinch of asaphoetida (hing),
  optional
300ml ($^1/_2$ pint), passata
75g ($2^1/_2$ oz) creamed
  coconut, cut into small pieces
1-2 fresh green chillies, seeded
450ml (15 fl oz) warm water
$1^1/_2$ teaspoons salt or to taste
15-30g ($^1/_2$-1 oz) sugar

Preparation time: 5-10 minutes
Cooking time: 5-10 minutes

1. Heat the oil over a medium heat and add the mustard seeds. As soon as they pop, add the curry leaves and asaphoetida (hing) and fry for 15 seconds.
2. Add the passata, coconut, green chillies and water. Bring to a slow simmer and stir until the coconut is dissolved.
3. Remove from the heat and allow to cool slightly. Blend the soup in a food processor or blender until the curry leaves and chillies are very finely chopped.
4. Return the pan to the heat and add the salt and sugar. Simmer for 5 minutes. Remove from the heat and serve.

Suitable for freezing.

Tomato and Coconut Soup

Sopa de Camrao
(Prawn Soup)
SERVES 4

A simple but richly flavoured soup which needs a good stock as a base. You can ask your fishmonger for off-cuts of various fish which make an excellent stock with a few added flavouring agents. Use the stock immediately as it will not keep, or freeze it.

For the stock:

2 litres (3½ pints) water

500g (1 lb) off-cuts of fish

1 large onion, approx. 250g (8 oz), unpeeled, washed and quartered

8 cloves of garlic, unpeeled and lightly crushed

1 teaspoon black peppercorns

5cm (2 inch) cube of fresh root ginger, unpeeled and sliced

2 carrots, unpeeled, washed and cut into thick slices

1 tablespoon coriander seeds

For the soup:

30g (1 oz) butter

1 small onion, approx. 125g (4 oz), finely chopped

2-3 cloves garlic, peeled and crushed

125g (4 oz) potatoes, finely chopped

½ teaspoon sweet paprika

600ml (1 pint) fish stock

180g (6 oz) cooked peeled prawns, or frozen prawns thawed and drained

100ml (3½ fl oz) single cream

½ teaspoon salt or to taste

¼ -½ teaspoon freshly milled black pepper

1 tablespoon chopped fresh parsley

Preparation time: 50-55 minutes including making stock

Cooking time: 20 minutes

To make the stock:

1. Put all the ingredients together in a large saucepan and bring to the boil. Cover and simmer for 45 minutes.

2. Line a sieve with fine muslin cloth and strain the stock.

To make the soup:

1. Melt the butter gently over a low heat in a heavy-based saucepan. Fry the onion and garlic until onion is soft but not brown. Add the potatoes and paprika and fry for 2-3 minutes.

2. Add the stock, bring to the boil, cover and simmer for 15 minutes or until the potatoes are tender.

3. Stir in half the prawns and remove from the heat. Allow to cool slightly. Reserve the remaining prawns.

4. Purée the soup in a blender or food processor and pour back into the saucepan. Add the cream, salt and pepper. Simmer gently for 5 minutes.

5. Stir in the parsley and reserved prawns and remove from the heat.

Serve with hot crusty rolls.

Unsuitable for freezing.

Smoked Mackerel Paté

SERVES 4

Smoked mackerels are very popular in Goa and most Goan housewives smoke the fish at home. The fish is wrapped in banana leaves and smoked over a wood fire or by covering with hay which is then set alight.

200g (7 oz) smoked mackerel
  fillets, skinned and flaked
1 fresh green chilli, seeded
1 small clove of garlic, peeled
  and chopped
2-3 tablespoons chopped fresh
  coriander leaves
150ml (5 fl oz) sour cream
60g (2 oz) finely chopped mild
  salad onion, red onion is
  ideal
4 teaspoons lime juice
salt and freshly milled black
  pepper to taste
½ a cucumber, sliced
2-3 firm ripe tomatoes, sliced
crisp lettuce leaves

Preparation time: 10-15 minutes
Cooking time: Nil

1. Put the mackerel, fresh chilli, garlic, coriander leaves and sour cream in a blender or food processor and blend until smooth.
2. Transfer to a mixing bowl and add the onions, lime juice, salt and pepper. Mix well and chill for two hours. You can leave it overnight in the fridge.
3. Put the mackerel paté, in a dish, in the middle of a flat serving plate and arrange cucumber, tomatoes and lettuce around it.

Serve with crusty rolls or crispbread. It is also good served on small savoury biscuits with drinks.

Unsuitable for freezing.

Broccoli Pakode
SERVES 4

*P*akode or Pakora can be made with any vegetable. A spicy batter made with chick-pea flour or 'Besan' is all you need to create mouth-watering Pakode. Besan has tiny lumps present in it, so should always be sieved before use.

1 small onion, approx. 125g (4 oz), coarsely chopped

2 cloves garlic, peeled

1cm (^{1}/2 inch) cube of fresh root ginger, peeled and chopped

1-2 fresh green chillies, seeded

15g (^{1}/2 oz) fresh coriander leaves including the tender stalks

1 teaspoon cummin seeds

2 teaspoons ground coriander

^{1}/4 teaspoon chilli powder, optional

^{1}/2 teaspoon salt or to taste

150g (5 oz) Besan (chick-pea flour), sieved

1 tablespoon ground rice

150ml (5 fl oz) water

Oil for deep frying

130g (4^1/2 oz) broccoli, cut into 1cm (^{1}/2 inch) florets

Preparation time: 20 minutes
Cooking time: 20 minutes

1. Put the onion, garlic, ginger, fresh chillies and fresh coriander in a blender or food processor. Add 2 tablespoons water and blend to a smooth purée.

2. Transfer the purée to a mixing bowl and add the cummin, coriander, chilli powder and salt. Mix well.

3. Add the Besan and ground rice. Gradually add the water, and mix until a smooth batter is formed.

4. Heat the oil over a medium heat. The temperature of the oil is crucial, so if you have a deep fat thermometer, heat the oil to 160°C (325°F). Or test the temperature by dropping a tiny amount of the batter into the oil. If the batter floats to the surface immediately without browning, then the oil is at the right temperature.

5. Dip each broccoli floret in the batter, making sure that it is fully coated. Fry the Pakode in the hot oil until they are golden brown, about 8-10 minutes. You need to brown them gently to make sure that the batter inside is cooked while the outside is crisp. Drain on absorbent paper.

Serve with chutney as a starter or with drinks. You can make a wonderful Pakode Platter by using cauliflower, broccoli and thickly sliced potatoes.

Suitable for freezing. After thawing, reheat under a low grill for about 6 minutes turning the Pakode over from time to time.

Broccoli Pakode served with a sliced onion and tomato salad.

Fish Cakes
MAKES 12

*Y*ou can use any white fish for these fish cakes; quite honestly expensive fish is a bit
of a waste as any fish tastes good when flavoured with a range of spices. I often
use skinned frozen coley steaks which are wonderful.

250g (8 oz) waxy potatoes,
   boiled, peeled and roughly
   chopped
400g (14 oz) steaks of any
   white fish, skinned and
   roughly chopped
2 tablespoons sunflower oil
1 medium onion, approx. 180g
   (6 oz), finely chopped
4 cloves garlic, peeled and
   crushed
2.5cm (1 inch) cube of fresh
   root ginger, peeled and grated
1-2 fresh green chillies, seeded
   and chopped
1/2 teaspoon ground turmeric
2 teaspoons ground coriander
1 teaspoon garam masala
1/2 teaspoon chilli powder,
   optional
15g (1/2 oz) fresh coriander
   leaves, finely chopped
1/2 teaspoon salt or to taste
30g (1 oz) plain flour
1 medium egg, beaten
90g (3 oz) soft white bread
   crumbs
Oil for frying

Preparation time: 30 minutes
Cooking time: 10-15 minutes

1. Put the potatoes and fish in a food processor
and blend to a coarse mixture using the pulse
action.
2. Heat the oil over a medium heat and fry the
onions until soft.
3. Add the garlic, ginger and fresh green chillies.
Stir and cook for 1 minute.
4. Add the turmeric, coriander, garam masala and
chilli powder, if used. Stir and cook for 1 minute.
5. Add the coriander leaves and salt. Stir and mix
well. Remove from the heat.
6. Put the fish and potato mixture in a large
mixing bowl and add the fried onions and spices.
Mix thoroughly. Cover the bowl and chill the mixture for at least 1 hour or overnight.
7. Divide the mixture into 12 equal-sized portions
and shape into flat round cakes about 1cm (1/2 inch)
thick.
8. Dust each cake in flour, then dip in beaten egg
and roll in breadcrumbs.
9. Heat a little oil in a frying pan over a medium
heat or use an electric deep fat fryer on a medium
setting. Fry the fish cakes until golden brown on
both sides. Drain on absorbent paper.

Serve as a starter with relishes or as a side dish with
Dali Ambat and plain boiled rice.

Suitable for freezing. Freeze the fish cakes fully
cooked.

Batata (Potato) Cutlets
MAKES 8

*G*oa *is noted for its excellent home produced cashews. For these yummy cutlets with cashews, I prepare the potato mixture a day or two in advance and store it in the fridge. They are delicious served hot with a relish of your choice. You can also make cocktail size cutlets or croquettes and serve them with drinks.*

625g (1¼ lb) old potatoes

90g (3 oz) unroasted shelled cashews

2 tablespoons sunflower oil

½ teaspoon black mustard seeds

½ teaspoon cummin seeds

1 medium onion, approx. 180g (6 oz), finely chopped

1-2 fresh green chillies, seeded and chopped

2 large cloves of garlic, peeled and crushed

1 teaspoon ground turmeric

¼-½ teaspoon chilli powder

1 teaspoon salt or to taste

15g (½ oz) chopped fresh coriander leaves, including the tender stalks

1 tablespoon lime juice

30g (1 oz) plain flour

1 medium egg, beaten

100g (3½ oz) soft white bread crumbs

Oil for frying

Preparation time: 30 minutes

Cooking time: 20 minutes

1. Boil the potatoes in their skins. Cool, peel and mash them.

2. Lightly crush the cashews with a rolling pin.

3. Heat the oil over a medium heat and add the mustard seeds. As soon as they begin to pop, add the cummin seeds and allow the seeds to crackle in the hot oil for a few seconds.

4. Add the onions, green chillies and garlic. Stir and fry until the onions are a pale golden colour.

5. Stir in the turmeric, chilli powder, salt and coriander leaves. Remove from the heat.

6. Add the mashed potato, cashews and lime juice to the onion mixture and mix thoroughly.

7. Divide the mixture into 8 equal-sized portions and shape into flat oval-shaped cutlets. Dust each cutlet in flour, then dip in beaten egg and roll in breadcrumbs.

8. Heat a little oil in a frying pan over a medium heat. You can also use an electric deep fat fryer if you wish. Fry the cutlets for about 5-7 minutes until golden brown and drain on absorbent paper.

Serve with a crisp salad for a light lunch or supper or as a starter with Brinjal Pickle.

Unsuitable for freezing.

Prawn Cutlets
MAKES 12

*Y*ou can use fresh or frozen prawns for these scrumptious cutlets. Most frozen prawns are peeled and cooked and are meant only to be eaten cold, but there are some which can be used in hot dishes. Read the information on the packaging to check whether the prawns are suitable for reheating.

2 slices of day or two old white bread
400g (14 oz) cooked peeled prawns
3 tablespoons sunflower oil
1 large onion, approx. 250g (8 oz), finely chopped
2 fresh green chillies, seeded and chopped
4 cloves garlic, peeled and crushed
2.5cm (1 inch) cube of fresh root ginger, peeled and finely grated
2 teaspoons ground coriander
1 teaspoon garam masala
$1/2$ teaspoon ground turmeric
$1/2$ teaspoon salt or to taste
$1/4$ teaspoon freshly milled black pepper
15g ($1/2$ oz) fresh coriander leaves, finely chopped
$1^1/2$ tablespoons lime juice
Oil for frying
30g (1 oz) plain flour
1 medium egg, beaten
90g (3 oz) soft white bread crumbs

Preparation time: 10-15 minutes
Cooking time: 20-25 minutes

1. Soak the bread in cold water for 5 minutes, squeeze out the water and blend in food processor until smooth, or mash with a fork.
2. Add the prawns to the processor bowl and using the pulse action, chop them coarsely. Alternatively, chop them with a knife.
3. Heat the oil over a medium heat and fry the onions, fresh chillies, garlic and ginger until the onions are soft, but not brown, about 6-8 minutes.
4. Add the coriander, garam masala and turmeric. Stir and fry for 1 minute. Add the salt, pepper and fresh coriander. Stir and cook for 30 seconds.
5. Add the prawn and bread mixture and lime juice. Remove from the heat and mix thoroughly. Put the mixture in a bowl, cover with plastic wrap and chill for at least 2 hours.
6. Pour the oil to approximately 2.5cm (1 inch) depth in a deep frying pan and heat over a medium heat.
7. Divide the prawn mixture into 12 and shape into oval cutlets. Dust each cutlet in flour, dip in beaten egg then roll in breadcrumbs. Fry in the hot oil until golden brown. Drain on absorbent paper.

Serve with chutney or serve as a main meal accompanied by Green Pullao and Cucumber Raita.

Suitable for freezing. Freeze only if fresh prawns are used

Prawn Cutlets with Cucumber Raita

Goan Pork Pies

MAKES 20 PIES

These lovely little pork pies are ideal for picnics and buffet parties. The minced pork for the filling is generously spiced and can be prepared in advance.

For the filling:

2 tablespoons sunflower oil
1 teaspoon cummin seeds
1 medium onion, approx. 180g
  (6 oz), finely chopped
2¹/₂ teaspoons minced or grated
  fresh root ginger
2¹/₂ teaspoons minced garlic
1-2 fresh green chillies, seeded
  and chopped

*Grind the following 7
ingredients together*

1-2 long slim, dried red chillies,
  chopped
¹/₂ teaspoon black peppercorns
1 cinnamon stick, 5cm
  (2 inch), broken up
6 whole cloves
6 green cardamoms
2 teaspoons cummin seeds
2 teaspoons coriander seeds

500g (1 lb) minced pork
1 teaspoon salt
1 teaspoon sugar
90ml (3 fl oz) warm water
2 tablespoons cider vinegar
180g (6 oz) chopped canned
  tomatoes, including the juice
2 tablespoons chopped fresh
  coriander leaves
1 quantity of Rich Goan Pastry,
  see opposite
1 egg yolk, beaten

Preparation time: 1 hour 15 minutes
Cooking time: 35-40 minutes

1. Heat the oil over a medium heat and add the cummin seeds. When they begin to crackle, add the onions and fry until soft but not brown.
2. Add the ginger, garlic and green chillies. Stir and fry for 1 minute. Add the ground ingredients. Stir and fry for 1 minute.
3. Add the pork, salt and sugar. Stir and fry the pork for 5-6 minutes over a medium heat.
4. Add the water, vinegar and tomatoes. Bring to the boil, cover and simmer for 15 minutes. The mixture should be moist not wet, so cook uncovered, if necessary, to reduce liquid.
5. Stir in the coriander leaves and remove from heat. Allow to become completely cold.
6. Brush a 12 section muffin tin with sunflower oil. Preheat the oven to 200C, 400F, Gas Mark 6
7. Divide the pastry into 4 and roll out each portion into a 25cm (10 inch) disc. Keep the remaining portions covered until required. Using a pastry cutter, 9cm (3¹/₂ inches) in diameter, cut out the required number of rounds and line the muffin tins.
8. Fill each muffin tin with a tablespoon of the minced pork and moisten the edges with water.
9. Cut out the same number of lids, approx. 7.5cm (3 inches) in diameter, and moisten the undersides with water. Place them on top of the filled pies. Press the edges lightly together, brush each pie with egg yolk and make two small slits in each one. Bake in the oven for about 15 minutes.

Suitable for freezing. Freeze the uncooked pies before baking.

Rich Goan Pastry
MAKES 750g (1½ lbs)

A rich pastry made with butter and eggs, this dough is very tolerant and does not mind being kneaded and rolled, so it is excellent for making little savouries such as Goan Pork Pies (see opposite).

400g (14 oz) self-raising flour or plain flour sieved with 1 teaspoon baking powder
1 teaspoon salt
1 tablespoon caster sugar
1 teaspoon caraway seeds
125g (4 oz) butter, melted
3 medium eggs, beaten

1. To make the pastry, put the flour, salt, sugar and caraway seeds into a large mixing bowl and mix thoroughly.
2. Add the melted butter and eggs and mix until a stiff dough is formed. Knead the dough until it feels smooth. Cover with a damp cloth or put into a plastic food bag and set aside for 30 minutes.
3. You can, of course, make the dough in the food processor if you wish. Just put all the ingredients in together and process with the pulse action until a smooth dough is formed. Leave to rest as in step 2. Use as required.

FISH
AND SEAFOOD

Prawn Cake

SERVES 4

*P*rawn Cake is an interesting concept. A spicy prawn filling is used between thin layers of egg pancakes. When I was served this in Goa, the whole cake was covered with mayonnaise to make it look like an iced cake. I have, however, left it plain but if you wish to 'ice' the cake, you could use low fat fromage frais, mayonnaise or sour cream.

For the filling:
200g (7 oz) cooked peeled prawns
2 tablespoons sunflower oil
1 medium onion, approx. 180g (6 oz), finely chopped
1cm (¹/₂ inch) cube of fresh root ginger, peeled and finely grated
3 cloves garlic, peeled and minced
3 teaspoons ground coriander
¹/₂ teaspoon ground cummin
¹/₂ teaspoon ground cinnamon
¹/₄ teaspoon ground cloves
¹/₄ -¹/₂ teaspoon chilli powder
90g (3 oz) chopped canned tomatoes with their juice
60g (2 oz) frozen garden peas, thawed or cooked fresh peas
¹/₂ teaspoon salt or to taste
1 tablespoon tomato purée
60g (2 oz) sour cream
For the pancakes:
6 medium eggs
salt and pepper to taste
sunflower oil for cooking

shredded lettuce leaves,
1 sweet red pepper, seeded, cut into rings and halved

Previous pages: Rochar and Prawn Cake

Preparation time: 20-25 minutes
Cooking time: 10-15 minutes

1. Chop the prawns finely.
2. Heat the oil over a medium heat and fry the onions until they are soft but not brown. Add the ginger and garlic and fry for 1 minute. Add the coriander, cummin, cinnamon, cloves and chilli powder and fry for 1 minute.
3. Add half the tomatoes and cook until the liquid evaporates. Add the remaining tomatoes and cook for 2 minutes. Add the prawns, peas, salt and tomato purée. Stir and cook for 2-3 minutes. Remove from the heat and cool thoroughly.
4. To make the pancakes, beat the eggs and season. In a 15cm (6 inch) frying pan, preferably non-stick, heat 1 teaspoon oil over a medium-low heat. Add 2 tablespoons egg and spread it quickly over the base of the pan. Allow to set and brown then turn over and brown the other side.
5. Make the remaining pancakes the same way. Pile them on top of one another, placing a piece of kitchen towel between each one.
6. Put a pancake on a dish. Spread with a little filling and top with another pancake. Continue layering in this way. Arrange the lettuce and peppers around the cake and serve.

Serve with boiled new potatoes.

Unsuitable for freezing.

Rochar
(Goan Stuffed Mackerel)
SERVES 4

*I*n Goa, a fish similar to mackerel, called 'Bhangra' is used for this lovely recipe. These are caught every morning and cooked on the same day because like all oily fish, they should be eaten absolutely fresh.

4 small mackerel, total weight
  1.25kg (2$^{1}/_{2}$ lb) gutted,
  cleaned, heads, fins and back
  bones removed
$^{1}/_{2}$ teaspoon salt
1 tablespoon lime juice
15g ($^{1}/_{2}$ oz) desiccated coconut
90ml (3 fl oz) very hot water
4 cloves garlic, peeled and
  chopped
2.5cm (1 inch) cube of fresh
  root ginger, peeled and
  chopped
1-2 fresh green chillies, seeded
  and chopped
1 dried red chilli, chopped
1$^{1}/_{2}$ teaspoons tamarind
  concentrate or 2 tablespoons
  lime juice
1 teaspoon ground cummin
$^{1}/_{2}$ teaspoon salt or to taste
Oil for frying
Seasoned flour:
45g (1$^{1}/_{2}$ oz) plain flour,
$^{1}/_{4}$ teaspoon salt
$^{1}/_{4}$ teaspoon freshly milled black
  pepper

Preparation time: 30 minutes
Cooking time: 10-12 minutes

1. Put the fish on a large plate, skin side down and gently rub in the salt and lime juice on the upper side. Set aside for 30 minutes.
2. Soak the coconut in hot water and set aside for 10 minutes.
3. Place the coconut and water, garlic, ginger, fresh and dried chillies, tamarind or lime juice, cummin and salt in a blender or food processor and make a smooth purée. Divide this purée into four equal portions and spread it on the fish, leaving about 5mm ($^{1}/_{4}$ inch) border. This stuffing is quite generous so don't worry if it appears over-stuffed, the flour used later will soak up any extra stuffing.
4. Tie the fish up with cotton or twine in a criss-cross pattern so that the stuffing is held intact.
5. Pour a little oil over the base of a large frying pan, preferably with a non-stick surface, and heat over a medium heat.
6. On a large plate, mix the flour, salt and pepper together. Coat each fish generously with the seasoned flour and fry until golden brown on both sides, about 10-12 minutes. Drain on absorbent paper.

Serve with plain boiled rice and Dhali Ambat.

Suitable for freezing. Freeze fully cooked.

Jhinga Caldeen
(Goan Prawn Curry)
SERVES 4

*G*oan cuisine is well-known for its excellent range of fish and seafood based *recipes. This dish combined with rice, is what most Goans live on. Caldeen is probably the mildest form of Goan curry. In this recipe any firm fish such as pomfret, monk fish, shark etc. may be used instead of prawns.*

400g (14 oz) fresh cooked, peeled prawns, (frozen prawns can be used if they are thawed and drained well)
$^1/_2$ teaspoon salt
2 tablespoons white wine or cider vinegar
1 teaspoon ground cummin
2 teaspoons ground coriander
1 teaspoon ground turmeric
$^1/_4$ -$^1/_2$ teaspoon chilli powder
$^1/_2$ teaspoon freshly milled black pepper
3 tablespoons sunflower oil
1 small onion, approx. 125g (4 oz), finely chopped
2.5cm (1 inch) cube fresh root ginger, peeled and grated
4 large or 6 small cloves garlic, peeled and crushed
250ml (8 fl oz) warm water
2-4 fresh green chillies, seeded and sliced lengthwise
$^1/_2$ teaspoon salt or to taste
90g (3 oz) creamed coconut, cut into small pieces
2 tablespoons chopped fresh coriander leaves

Preparation time: 15 minutes
Cooking time: 15 minutes

1. Put the prawns in a mixing bowl and add the salt and vinegar. Stir and mix well. Set aside for 10-15 minutes.
2. Mix the cummin, coriander, turmeric, chilli powder, and black pepper in a small bowl and set aside.
3. Heat the oil over a medium heat and fry the onions gently until they are a pale golden colour, about 8-9 minutes. Stir constantly.
4. Add the ginger and garlic and fry for 1 minute.
5. Add the mixed ground spices and fry for 1-2 minutes.
6. Add the water, fresh green chillies, salt and coconut. Simmer until the coconut is dissolved.
7. Add the prawns and cook for 2-5 minutes. This will depend on the type of prawns used; standard prawns, King prawns, Tiger prawns etc.
8. Add half the chopped coriander leaves and remove from the heat. Put the prawns in a serving dish and garnish with the remaining chopped coriander leaves.

Serve with plain boiled rice or Garlic Rice accompanied by Vegetable Stew.

Suitable for freezing. Freeze only if fresh prawns are used

Jhinga Caldeen with Garlic Rice.

Baked Salmon
SERVES 4-8

When whole salmon are down in price I buy and freeze them so that I can make this delicious baked dish any time. In Goa, a fish known as 'Surmai' is dubbed 'Indian Salmon' because it is similar in appearance, texture and flavour.

1 fresh salmon, total weight
  1.25 kg (2½ lb) head on,
  cleaned, gutted and backbone
  removed
2 tablespoons lime juice
½ teaspoon salt
3 tablespoons sunflower oil
1 medium onion, approx. 150g
  (5 oz), finely chopped
4 cloves garlic, peeled and
  crushed
4 teaspoons ground coriander
½ teaspoon chilli powder
¼ teaspoon ground turmeric
30g (1 oz) creamed coconut,
  cut into small pieces
180g (6 oz) fresh, cooked,
  peeled prawns
1 tablespoon finely chopped
  fresh coriander leaves
1½ tablespoons tomato purée
½ teaspoon salt or to taste
½ cucumber, sliced
2-3 firm tomatoes, sliced
shredded crisp lettuce

Preparation time: 30 minutes
Cooking time: 50-55 minutes

1. Make 3 deep slashes on each side of the salmon. These slits are to hold some of the filling.
2. Rub the lime juice all over the fish, and sprinkle with the salt. Set aside for 30 minutes.
3. Heat the oil over a medium heat and fry the onions until soft but not brown. Add the garlic and coriander. Stir and fry for 1 minute. Add the chilli powder and turmeric. Fry for 30 seconds. Add 2 tablespoons water and cook until the water evaporates. Repeat the process once more.
4. Add the creamed coconut, prawns, coriander leaves, tomato purée and salt. Reduce the heat to low and stir until the coconut has dissolved. Remove from the heat and cool thoroughly.
5. Preheat the oven to 180°C, 350°F, Gas Mark 4. Fill the stomach cavity of the salmon with some of the stuffing and fold the sides together. Use remaining stuffing to fill the 6 slashes.
6. Wrap the stuffed salmon loosely in a piece of lightly oiled foil. Place in a deep roasting tin and bake in the oven for 20 minutes. Fold back the foil and turn the temperature up to 190°C, 375°F, Gas Mark 5 and bake for 20 minutes. Remove and let the fish rest for 15-20 minutes.
7. Place on a serving dish and surround with cucumber, tomatoes and lettuce.

Serve with boiled new potatoes.

Suitable for freezing. Freeze fully cooked if fresh prawns are used.

Fish Ambot Tik
(Fish in a hot and sour sauce)
SERVES 4

*F*ish *is a very popular item in Goa, especially among the Hindu community who, as in several other parts of India, are strict vegetarians. There is an abundance of fish and seafood due to Goa's extended coastline and the network of inland waterways.*

750g (1½ lb) steaks of shark or monk fish
1 tablespoon cider vinegar
1 teaspoon salt
1 teaspoon ground turmeric
3 tablespoons coconut, vegetable or corn oil
1 tablespoon minced or crushed garlic
1 small onion, approx. 125g (4 oz), finely chopped
1 tablespoon ground coriander
½-1 teaspoon chilli powder
2 teaspoons sweet paprika
90g (3oz) creamed coconut, cut into small pieces
300ml (½ pint) warm water
1 level teaspoon tamarind concentrate or 1½ table spoons lemon juice

Preparation time: 20 minutes plus marinating
Cooking time: 15 minutes

1. Skin the shark or monk fish and divide each steak into two by cutting along the centre bone.
2. Wash the fish gently and drain. Lay the fish on a large plate and pour the vinegar evenly over it. Sprinkle with half the salt and half the turmeric. Turn the pieces of fish over with a spoon until the turmeric and salt are evenly distributed. Cover and set aside for 20 minutes.
3. Heat the oil over a medium heat and add the garlic. Allow garlic to brown lightly, then add the onions and fry until the onions are soft but not brown, about 5 minutes. Stir frequently. Add the ground coriander. Stir and fry for 1 minute.
4. Mix the remaining turmeric, chilli powder and paprika in a small bowl and add 2 tablespoons of water to make a paste. Add this to the pan, reduce heat to low and cook for 1-2 minutes
5. Add the coconut, water, tamarind and the remaining salt. Stir until the coconut and tamarind are dissolved. If you are using lemon juice simply stir this in at the end of the cooking time.
6. Add the fish along with all the juices and bring it to a slow simmer. Cover the pan and simmer gently for 5 minutes. Remove from the heat and serve.

Serve with plain boiled rice and Vegetable Stew.

Suitable for freezing.

Mashli Ghashi
SERVES 4

This is a delicious fish curry created by the Goan Hindus. My mother-in-law excels herself every time she cooks this curry. I have adapted the recipe to suit a busy life-style. The traditional cooking medium for this recipe is coconut oil which you can buy from Indian grocers. Vegetable or corn oil will, however, produce perfectly good results.

750g (1¹/₂ lb) steaks of salmon, monk fish or shark
1 teaspoon salt
60ml (2 fl oz) coconut, vegetable or corn oil
1 medium onion, approx. 180g (6 oz), finely chopped
5 large or 8 small cloves garlic, peeled and crushed
4 teaspoons ground coriander
¹/₂-1 teaspoon chilli powder
1 teaspoon ground turmeric
60g (2 oz) coconut milk powder
250ml (8 fl oz) hot water
1 teaspoon tamarind concentrate or 1¹/₂ table spoons lime juice

Preparation time: 30 minutes
Cooking time: 20 minutes

1. Remove the scales from the fish, but leave the skin on. Halve the steaks lengthwise and lay them on a large plate in a single layer. Sprinkle half the salt on the steaks and set aside for 20 minutes.
2. Heat the oil over a medium heat in a wide, shallow pan large enough to hold the fish in a single layer. Add the onions and fry until they are a pale golden colour, 8-9 minutes. Stir frequently.
3. Add the garlic and fry for 30 seconds.
4. Add the coriander and fry for 1 minute, stirring constantly.
5. Stir in the chilli powder and turmeric.
6. Blend the coconut milk powder with the hot water and add to the spices.
7. Add the tamarind or lime juice, and remaining salt and simmer gently for 2-3 minutes or until tamarind has dissolved.
8. Arrange the fish in the pan in a single layer. Cover and simmer for 5 minutes. Turn the fish over, re-cover and simmer for a further 5 minutes. Remove from the heat and serve.

Serve with plain boiled rice, Mung Bean Usal and a carrot salad.

Suitable for freezing.

Mashli Ghashi with fresh carrot salad.

Prawns à la Goa
SERVES 4

*P*rawns steeped in a rich tomato and onion sauce look absolutely fabulous and taste as good as they look. I had this in Goa where they used the huge Tiger Prawns found locally. I have, however, used good quality fresh prawns which are also delicious cooked this way. Any firm white fish may be used in this recipe in place of the prawns.

400g (14 oz) fresh, cooked, peeled prawns
¼ teaspoon salt
1 tablespoon cider vinegar
90ml (3 fl oz) sunflower oil
2 large onions, approx. 400g (14 oz), finely sliced
8 large cloves of garlic, peeled and minced or crushed
2.5cm (1 inch) cube of fresh root ginger, peeled and finely grated
3 teaspoons ground coriander
1 teaspoon ground cummin
1 teaspoon ground turmeric
½ teaspoon chilli powder
¼ teaspoon ground cloves
½ teaspoon ground cinnamon
400g (14 oz) canned tomatoes, sieved or 300ml (½ pint) passata
45g (1½ oz) creamed coconut, cut into small pieces
30g (1 oz) coconut milk powder
250ml (8 fl oz) hot water
6-8 whole fresh green chillies
½ teaspoon salt or to taste
2 tablespoons chopped fresh coriander leaves

Preparation time: 15 minutes
Cooking time: 15-20 minutes

1. Put the prawns in a bowl and add the salt and vinegar. Mix well and set aside for 30 minutes.
2. Heat the oil over a medium heat and fry the onions until they are a light golden colour, about 8-10 minutes. Stir frequently.
3. Remove pan from the heat. Remove onions, draining off as much oil as possible.
4. Place the pan with the remaining oil over a low heat and fry the garlic and ginger for 1 minute.
5. Add the coriander, cummin, turmeric, chilli powder, cloves and cinnamon. Stir and fry for 1 minute when the spices will release their flavour.
6. Add the prawns, sieved tomatoes or passata and creamed coconut. Bring to a slow simmer and stir until the coconut has dissolved.
7. Blend the coconut milk powder with the hot water and add to the prawns. Cover and simmer for 5 minutes. If you are using Tiger Prawns allow 8-9 minutes.
8. Add the fresh whole chillies, salt and chopped coriander. Simmer for 2-3 minutes and remove from heat.

Serve with plain boiled rice and Batata Sukkhe or Broccoli Upkari.

Suitable for freezing if fresh prawns are used.

Fried Sardines
SERVES 4

Sardines are available almost throughout the year and they make excellent eating. Like all oily fish, they must be eaten absolutely fresh and despite being fiddley, the smaller ones are tastier.

16 Portuguese sardines, total weight 750g (1¹/₂ lb) scales and fins removed

2¹/₂ teaspoons tamarind concentrate or the juice of 1 lime

4 tablespoons water, (not necessary if you are using lime juice)

3 tablespoons chopped onions

4 cloves garlic, peeled and chopped

2-4 fresh green chillies, seeded and chopped

2 tablespoons chopped fresh coriander leaves

1 teaspoon salt or to taste

¹/₂ teaspoon ground turmeric

Oil for frying

2.5cm (1 inch) cube of fresh root ginger, unpeeled and sliced

2 dried red chillies, slit length wise and seeded

60g (2 oz) plain flour

¹/₄ teaspoon salt

¹/₄ teaspoon freshly milled black pepper

Preparation time: 30 minutes
Cooking time: 15-20 minutes

1. Leave the heads on the fish and slit along the bellies and remove the guts. Wash gently under running water, making sure that you remove any black bits. Drain and dry thoroughly.

2. Put the tamarind and water or lime juice, onions, garlic, fresh chillies and coriander leaves in a blender or food processor and blend until smooth. Transfer the mixture to a bowl and stir in the salt and turmeric.

3. Put the sardines on a large plate and pour the marinade over. Turn the fish thoroughly until all sides of the sardines are coated. Cover with plastic food wrap, then leave to marinate for 1 hour.

4. To make a flavoured oil pour about 2.5cm (1 inch) oil into a deep frying pan and heat over a medium heat. Add the ginger and red chillies. Fry until the ginger is well browned and the chillies are blackened. Remove them with a slotted spoon and discard.

5. Mix the flour, salt and pepper together. Coat each sardine generously with seasoned flour and fry in batches in the flavoured oil for 2-3 minutes on each side or until they are golden brown. Drain on absorbent paper.

Serve with Garlic Rice and Masala Dhal.

Unsuitable for freezing.

Prawn Pie
(Apa de camrao)
SERVES 4

*A*wonderful combination of texture, and an imaginative and most creative way to use local Goan produce. This pie is topped with a very unusual batter-type pastry.

For the filling:

3 tablespoons sunflower oil
1 medium onion, approx. 180g
  (6 oz), finely chopped
1-2 fresh green chillies, seeded
  and chopped
4 cloves garlic, peeled and
  minced
2.5cm (1 inch) cube fresh root
  ginger, peeled and finely
  grated
1 teaspoon ground cummin
3 teaspoons ground coriander
$^1/_4$ -$^1/_2$ teaspoon chilli powder
$^1/_2$ teaspoon ground turmeric
1 teaspoon garam masala
350g (12 oz) fresh, cooked,
  peeled prawns, or frozen
  prawns thawed, drained and
  dried
1 teaspoon salt or to taste
1 tablespoon tomato purée
45g (1$^1/_2$ oz) creamed coconut,
  cut into small pieces
1 teaspoon sugar
2 tablespoons chopped fresh
  coriander leaves
1 tablespoon cider vinegar
1 quantity Goan Rice and
  Coconut Pastry, see page 48
sunflower oil or melted butter
  for glazing

Preparation time: 25 minutes, not including pastry
Cooking time: 45 minutes

1. Heat the oil over a medium heat and fry the onions and green chillies until soft. Add the garlic and ginger. Stir and fry for 1 minute. Add the cummin and coriander. Stir and fry for 1 minute. Add the chilli powder, turmeric and garam masala. Stir and fry for 30 seconds.
2. Add two tablespoons of water. Stir and cook until the water evaporates. Repeat once more.
3. Add the prawns, salt, tomato purée, coconut and sugar. Stir and cook gently until coconut has dissolved. Stir in the coriander leaves and vinegar and remove from the heat. Allow to become cold.
4. Make the Rice and Coconut Pastry.
5. Preheat the oven to 180°C, 350°F, Gas Mark 4. Line the base of a 28 x 18cm (11 x 7 inch) roasting tin with non-stick baking parchment and brush the sides with oil. Pour half the pastry batter evenly over the base. Cook in the centre of the oven until just set, about 5-6 minutes.
6. Remove the tin from the oven and spread the prawn mixture evenly over the crust. Spread the remaining batter completely over the filling. Return to the oven and bake for 5 minutes.
7. Brush the top of the pie with oil or melted butter. Bake for 15-20 minutes or until crisp and golden brown.

Serve hot or cold with a crisp mixed salad.

Unsuitable for freezing.

Prawn Pie with green salad.

Goan Rice and Coconut Pastry.
MAKES 350G (12 OZ)

This pastry is made with ground rice, which the Goans first allow to ferment with 'Toddy', the coconut vinegar (See Glossary.) I have used easy-blend yeast to aid fermentation.

300g (10 oz) ground rice

60g (2 oz) desiccated coconut, finely ground in a coffee grinder

3 teaspoons easy-blend dried yeast

$^1/_2$ teaspoon salt

$^1/_2$ teaspoon sugar

$^1/_4$ teaspoon freshly milled black pepper

300ml ($^1/_2$ pint) lukewarm water

5 egg yolks

1. To make the pastry, mix together the ground rice, coconut, yeast, salt, sugar and pepper in a large mixing bowl. Gradually add the water. Make sure the water is just lukewarm and not hot. Mix until a thick batter is formed and let it cool completely.

2. Beat the egg yolks together and add to the rice mixture. Mix well. Rinse a metal or steel bowl, or saucepan, with warm water and transfer the batter. Metal or steel will retain heat better and therefore help to ferment the mixture. Cover the bowl or saucepan and leave it in a warm place for 1-1$^1/_2$ hours. Use as required for Prawn Pie, page 46

Prawn and Egg Baffad

SERVES 4

There is no doubt that prawns in the shell are much more delicious than the pre-peeled ones. They are lovely and fun to eat if you are going to cook them in the shell. But I like to buy the fresh peeled, ready-to-cook variety for cooking Indian style.

4 hard-boiled eggs
75ml (2½ fl oz) sunflower oil
1 large onion, approx. 250g
 (8 oz), finely chopped
2 teaspoons ground coriander
1 teaspoon garam masala
½ teaspoon ground turmeric
½-1 teaspoon chilli powder
3.5cm (1½ inch) cube of fresh
 root ginger, peeled and finely
 grated
6 cloves of garlic, peeled and
 crushed or minced
125g (4 oz) chopped canned
 tomatoes with their juice
30g (1 oz) coconut milk
 powder
200ml (7 fl oz) hot water
250g (8 oz) fresh, cooked
 peeled prawns
½ teaspoon salt or to taste
1 tablespoon lime juice
sprigs of fresh coriander

Preparation time: 15-20 minutes
Cooking time: 25 minutes

1. Shell the eggs and using a sharp knife, make 4-5 slits lengthwise on each egg without cutting them through.
2. Heat the oil over a medium heat and fry the onion until soft but not brown.
3. Mix the coriander, garam masala, turmeric, chilli powder, ginger and garlic in a small bowl and add 3 tablespoons water to make a paste. Add spice paste to the onions and cook for 1-2 minutes. Reduce heat to low and continue to cook for a further 3-4 minutes.
4. Add half the tomatoes and cook for 2-3 minutes. Add remaining tomatoes and cook for a further 2-3 minutes.
5. Blend the coconut milk powder with the hot water and add to the spices. Add the prawns, salt and eggs. Bring to a slow simmer and cook gently for 5 minutes.
6. Add the lime juice and remove from the heat.
7. Transfer the eggs to a plate and put the prawns in a serving dish. Halve the eggs lengthwise and arrange on top of the prawns with sprigs of fresh coriander.

Serve with plain boiled rice and Vegetable Stew

Suitable for freezing only if fresh prawns are used.

CHICKEN

Chicken Chacuti
SERVES 4

I remember this dish as the highlight of a meal in the Beach Hut at the Taj Village Hotel in Goa. The chef willingly gave me his recipe and here is my version.

750g (1½ lb) skinned chicken joints, either leg or breast
½ teaspoon salt
4 tablespoons lime juice
60g (2 oz) desiccated coconut
1 teaspoon black mustard seeds
4 whole cloves
Two 2.5cm (1 inch) pieces cassia bark or cinnamon stick, broken up
½ teaspoon fenugreek seeds
2-6 dried red chillies, chopped
1 tablespoon white poppy seeds
30g (1 oz) roasted salted peanuts
4 tablespoons sunflower oil
1 large onion, approx. 250g (8 oz), finely chopped
3.5cm (1½ inch) cube of fresh root ginger, peeled and grated
6 large cloves of garlic, peeled and crushed
½ teaspoon ground turmeric
1 tablespoon ground coriander
1 teaspoon ground fennel
½ teaspoon ground nutmeg
250ml (8 fl oz) warm water
½ teaspoon salt or to taste
1-2 fresh green chillies, seeded and sliced lengthwise
2 tablespoons cider vinegar

Preparation time: 30-35 minutes
Cooking time: 55-60 minutes

1. Cut each chicken joint into two, rub in the salt and lime juice and set aside for 30 minutes.
2. Preheat a heavy-based frying pan over a medium heat. Reduce the heat to low and add the coconut, and roast until lightly browned, about 2-3 minutes. Stir well. Transfer to a dish and cool.
3. Place the pan back on low heat and roast the mustard seeds, cloves, cassia or cinnamon, fenugreek and red chillies. Stir, and when the seeds start crackling, put on a dish and cool.
4. Grind the roasted coconut, the roasted spices, the poppy seeds and peanuts. Mix the ground ingredients, and add enough water to make a paste.
5. Heat the oil over medium heat in a heavy-based pan, add the onions, and fry until pale golden.
6. Add the ginger and garlic. Stir and fry for 1 minute. Add the turmeric, coriander, fennel and nutmeg. Stir and fry for 1 minute. Add the spice paste. Stir and fry for 4-5 minutes.
7. Add the chicken, and fry for 8-10 minutes over a medium heat, stirring frequently.
8. Add the water and salt and bring to the boil. Cover and simmer until the chicken is tender; 45-50 minutes for leg, 25 minutes for breast.
9. Add the fresh green chillies and vinegar. Cover and simmer for 5 minutes, then serve.

Serve with plain boiled rice and Batata Ghashi or Cauliflower Ambat.

Suitable for freezing.

Previous pages: Rice Chapatties, Chicken Chacuti and Fried Chilli Chicken.

Fried Chilli Chicken
SERVES 4

Marinated chicken thighs, first cooked in their own juices, then fried gently in a little ghee or butter which lends a very enticing flavour and appearance.

1kg (2 lb) chicken thighs, skinned

1/2 teaspoon salt

4 teaspoons lime juice

1 small onion, approx. 125g (4 oz), chopped

4 large or 6 small cloves of garlic, peeled and chopped

5cm (2 inch) piece of fresh root ginger, peeled and chopped

1-2 fresh green chillies, seeded

75ml (2 fl oz) cider vinegar

Grind the following 6 ingredients until fine:

2 teaspoons coriander seeds

1 teaspoon cummin seeds

1-2 long slim dried red chillies, chopped

5cm (2 inch) piece of cassia bark or 2.5cm (1 inch) cinnamon stick, broken up

4 whole cloves

4 green cardamoms

4 teaspoons ghee or unsalted butter

1/2 teaspoon salt or to taste

4 teaspoons sugar

4 teaspoons tomato purée

6 whole fresh green chillies, seeded and sliced

2 tablespoons chopped fresh coriander leaves

Preparation time: 20 minutes plus marinating

Cooking time: 50 minutes

1. Put the chicken in a large bowl or plastic tub and rub in the salt and lime juice. Cover and set aside for 30 minutes.

2. Purée the onions, garlic, ginger and green chillies with the vinegar in a blender until smooth. Add the ground spices and blend again.

3. Pour the spice mixture over the chicken. Stir and mix thoroughly. Cover and leave to marinate for 4-6 hours or overnight in the fridge. Remove from the fridge 30 minutes before cooking.

4. Put the chicken, along with any extra marinade left in the bowl, in a large pan over a medium heat. Cover the pan and simmer the chicken in its own juices for 40 minutes. Stir occasionally.

5. Remove the lid and continue to cook until the liquid evaporates and a thick paste is formed. Stir frequently.

6. Add the ghee or butter, salt and sugar and fry the chicken until well browned, about 10 minutes.

7. Add the tomato purée, fresh chillies and coriander leaves. Stir and fry for 2 minutes and remove from heat. The thick spice paste should coat the chicken when finished.

Serve with Cauliflower Pullao and Masala Dhal.

Suitable for freezing.

Chicken Cafreal
SERVES

*T*his is a hot and spicy dish, for which you will need to make the marinade recipe on page 56. Boned chicken, cut into large pieces, can be used instead of joints.

750g (1½ lb) skinned chicken joints, use either leg or breast but not both
1 quantity of Hot and Spicy Paste, see page 56
60ml (2 fl oz) sunflower oil
1cm (½ inch) cube of fresh root ginger, peeled and cut into julienne sticks
1 medium onion, approx. 180g (6 oz), finely chopped
250ml (8 fl oz) warm water
100g (3½ oz) creamed coconut, cut into small pieces
1 teaspoon salt or to taste
15g (½ oz) fresh coriander leaves, chopped

Preparation time: 20 minutes
Cooking time: 50 minutes

1. Cut each chicken joint into two by separating leg from thigh, or by cutting the breast into two pieces widthwise.
2. Put the chicken in a large bowl and add the Hot and Spicy Paste. Mix until each piece is thoroughly coated. Cover and put in the fridge for at least 3-4 hours. Remove from the fridge 30 minutes before cooking.
3. Heat half the oil over a medium heat. Add the chicken and and fry for 2 minutes. Cover the pan tightly and reduce the heat to low. Let the chicken cook in its own juices for 25-30 minutes for leg portions, 20 minutes for breast and 15 minutes for boned pieces.
4. Turn the heat up to medium and cook, uncovered, for 3-4 minutes or until the juice reduces to a paste-like consistency. In a separate pan, heat the remaining oil and fry the ginger julienne for 30 seconds.
5. Add the onions and fry until they are soft but not brown, about 5 minutes.
6. Add the chicken, water, coconut and salt. Bring to the boil, reduce heat and stir until coconut is dissolved. Cover the pan and simmer for 4-5 minutes. Stir in the coriander leaves, remove from heat and serve.

Serve with Tomato Pullao and Broccoli Upkari.

Suitable for freezing.

Chicken Cafreal with Broccoli Upkari.

Hot and Spicy Paste

Goan curries tend to be rather hot; please adjust chillies according to your taste. Always remove the seeds if you prefer a mild sauce.

¹/₂ teaspoon black peppercorns
2-6 dried red chillies, chopped
1 teaspoon cummin seeds
1 teaspoon coriander seeds
5cm (2 inch) piece of cassia
  bark or cinnamon stick,
  broken up
4 green cardamom pods
4 whole cloves
2.5cm (1 inch) cube of fresh
  root ginger, peeled
4-6 cloves of garlic, peeled
1-4 fresh green chillies, seeded
juice of 1 lime

1. Using a coffee grinder, grind the peppercorns, red chillies, cummin, coriander, cassia or cinnamon, cardamom and cloves until very fine.
2. Chop the ginger, garlic and chillies and purée in a blender or food processor until smooth. Mix the ground spices with the puréed ingredients to make a paste. Use as required for Chicken Cafreal, page 54.

Vindaloo Spice Paste

In Goa, the spices are ground with 'Toddy' the vinegar made by fermenting the sap of the coconut palm. (See Glossary.) Cider vinegar works very well instead.

6 large cloves of garlic, peeled
3.5cm (1¹/₂ inch) cube of fresh
  root ginger, peeled
60ml (2 fl oz) cider vinegar
4 teaspoons coriander seeds
1¹/₂ teaspoons cummin seeds
1¹/₂ teaspoons black mustard
  seeds
1 teaspoon fenugreek seeds
2-4 dried red chillies, chopped
4 whole cloves
Two 5cm (2 inch) pieces of
  cassia bark or cinnamon stick
¹/₂ a whole nutmeg, crushed

1. Chop the garlic and ginger and purée with the vinegar in a blender.
2. Put the coriander, cummin, black mustard and fenugreek seeds into a coffee grinder and grind until fine. Grind the chillies, cloves, cassia or cinnamon and crushed nutmeg in the same way.
3. Mix the ground spices together and add to vinegar mixture in blender. Blend well. Use as required for Chicken Vindaloo, page 58.

Chicken Gizzad
SERVES 4

This is my favourite chicken dish; simple but superb! The fresh green chillies complement the fruity flavour of the coconut and cider vinegar beautifully. Coconut milk powder is available in most good supermarkets as well as Indian stores. Any curry which is coconut based thickens considerably in cooling. Do not boil to reduce the sauce even if it appears slightly watery. Coconut milk also curdles if boiled for too long.

750g (1½lb) chicken joints, skinned

4 tablespoons lime juice

½ teaspoon salt

60ml (2 fl oz) sunflower oil

1 large onion, approx. 250g (8 oz), finely sliced

4 large or 6 small cloves of garlic, peeled and crushed

3.5cm (1½ inch) cube of fresh root ginger, peeled and grated

Mix the following 5 ingredients in a small bowl:

1 teaspoon ground cinnamon

½ teaspoon freshly milled black pepper

2 teaspoons ground cummin

1 teaspoon ground turmeric

1 teaspoon sweet paprika

45g (1½ oz) coconut milk powder

300ml (½ pint) warm water

½ teaspoon salt or to taste

2-8 fresh green chillies, seeded and sliced lengthwise

2 tablespoons cider vinegar

Preparation time: 20 minutes plus marinating
Cooking time: 45-50 minutes

1. Cut each chicken joint into two by separating leg from thigh and cutting breast pieces into halves widthwise.

2. Rub the lime juice and salt into the chicken, cover and set aside for 30 minutes.

3. Heat the oil over a medium heat and fry the onions until they are soft, but not brown, about 5-6 minutes.

4. Add the garlic and ginger and fry for 1 minute.

5. Add 3 tablespoons water to the spice mixture and make a paste. Add to the pan and fry on low heat for 2-3 minutes, stirring constantly. Add 2 tablespoons water and cook until the water evaporates. Stir frequently. Repeat the process once more.

6. Add the chicken, stir and mix thoroughly. Cover the pan and reduce the heat to low. Cook the chicken in its own juice for 20-25 minutes.

7. Blend the coconut milk powder with the warm water and add to the chicken. Add the salt and green chillies, cover and simmer for 15 minutes.

8. Stir in the vinegar and serve.

Serve with Tomato Pullao or plain boiled rice accompanied by Aubergine Curry or Vegetable Stew.

Suitable for freezing.

Chicken Vindaloo
SERVES 4

*V*indaloo is a traditional, fiery hot Goan dish. Originally it was made with pork and potato but now the term Vindaloo has come to mean just a very hot dish.

750g (1½ lb) skinned chicken joints, use either leg or breast but not both

1 quantity of Vindaloo Spice Paste, see page 56

60ml (2 fl oz) sunflower oil

2 cloves garlic, peeled and crushed

1 teaspoon ground cummin

1 large onion, approx. 250g (8 oz), finely chopped

1 teaspoon sweet paprika

¼ -½ teaspoon chilli powder

½ teaspoon ground turmeric

180ml (6 fl oz) water

250g (8 oz) potatoes, peeled and cut into 5cm (2 inch) cubes

90ml (3 fl oz) dry white wine

90ml (3 fl oz) dry white wine

1¼ teaspoon salt or to taste

1 tablespoon cider vinegar

Preparation time: 20-25 minutes plus marinating
Cooking time: 1 hour 10 minutes

1. Cut each chicken joint into two by separating leg from thigh and cutting breast pieces into halves.
2. Put the chicken in a large bowl or plastic tub and add the Vindaloo Spice Paste. Mix thoroughly. Cover and leave to marinate for 5-6 hours or overnight in the fridge. Remove from the fridge 30 minutes before cooking.
3. Heat the oil over a medium heat in a heavy-based saucepan. Blend the crushed garlic and ground cummin with 1 tablespoon of water and add to the hot oil. Fry for 1 minute.
4. Add the onions and fry until they are soft but not brown.
5. Add the chicken. Adjust the heat to high and fry for 6-8 minutes, stirring frequently.
6. Add the paprika, chilli powder and turmeric. Stir and cook for 2 minutes.
7. Add the water and bring to the boil. Cover and simmer for 25 minutes.
8. Add the potatoes and salt. Cover and simmer for 15 minutes.
9. Add the wine. Cover and simmer for 10 minutes, or until the potatoes are tender.
10. Stir in the vinegar, remove from the heat and serve.

Serve with plain boiled rice, Mung Bean Usal and Carrot Raita.

Suitable for freezing if frozen before adding the potatoes.

Chicken Vindaloo with Brinjal Pickle.

Chicken Pot Roast
SERVES 4

A deliciously different way to serve a pot roast. The chicken is first browned in hot oil, then simmered gently in a rich, spiced tomato and onion sauce.

4 skinned chicken joints, total weight approx. 750g (1¹/₂ lb)

¹/₂ teaspoon salt

4 teaspoons lime juice

1 large onion, approx. 250g (8 oz), coarsely chopped

5cm (2 inch) cube of fresh root ginger, peeled and chopped

4 large or 6 small cloves of garlic, peeled

2 dried red chillies, chopped

125ml (4 fl oz) sunflower oil

350g (12 oz) small new potatoes, scrubbed and washed

2 teaspoons ground coriander

1 teaspoon ground turmeric

1 teaspoon garam masala

180g (6 oz) chopped canned tomatoes with juice

¹/₄ teaspoon chilli powder, optional

¹/₂ teaspoon salt or to taste

250ml (8 fl oz) warm water

2 tablespoons fresh coriander leaves, finely chopped

1 tablespoon cider vinegar

Preparation time: 30 minutes
Cooking time: 1 hour 20 minutes

1. Put the chicken in a bowl and rub in the salt and lime juice. Cover and leave for 30 minutes.
2. Purée the onion, ginger, garlic and red chillies in a blender, with 2 tablespoons water, until smooth.
3. Heat the oil over a medium-high heat in a large heavy-based pan. Add the chicken and fry until golden brown. Drain.
4. Add the potatoes and fry until they are golden brown. Drain.
5. Add the puréed ingredients to the remaining oil. Stir and fry for about 8-10 minutes.
6. Add the coriander, turmeric and garam masala. Stir and fry for 2 minutes. Add half the tomatoes and cook for 2-3 minutes. Add the remaining tomatoes and chilli powder, if used. Stir and cook until the oil is visible again.
7. Add the salt and water and mix well. Lay the chicken joints on the sauce. Cover and simmer for 20 minutes.
8. Add the potatoes. Cover and simmer for 20-25 minutes or until tender. Remove the lid and simmer until the sauce resembles a thick batter. Add half the coriander leaves and vinegar. Stir and mix well. Remove from the heat.
9. Sprinkle with the remaining coriander leaves and serve.

Serve with Chapatties and chutney.

Suitable for freezing.

Chicken Baffad

SERVES 4

*G*oa's climate is ideal for growing coconut; hence the extensive use of this versatile fruit in Goan cuisine. For this recipe, traditionally, fresh coconut is grated and the milk is extracted twice. The first extraction is known as thick coconut milk and the second as thin coconut milk. However, you can achieve a wonderful rich flavour by using coconut milk powder and creamed coconut.

750g (1¹/₂ lb) chicken joints, skinned and halved

¹/₂ teaspoon salt

4 teaspoons lime juice

60ml (2 fl oz) sunflower oil

1 large onion, approx. 250g (8 oz), finely sliced

Mix the following 7 ingredients

¹/₂-1 teaspoon chilli powder

1 teaspoon ground turmeric

1 teaspoon ground cinnamon

¹/₂ teaspoon ground cloves

1 teaspoon ground cummin

1 teaspoon sweet paprika

¹/₂ teaspoon milled black pepper

6 cloves of fresh garlic, peeled and crushed

3.5cm (1¹/₂ inch) cube of fresh root ginger, peeled and finely grated

180ml (6 fl oz) warm water

45g (1¹/₂ oz) coconut milk powder

90ml (3 fl oz) hot water

30g (1 oz) creamed coconut cut into small pieces

¹/₂ teaspoon salt or to taste

4 whole fresh green chillies

2 tablespoons cider vinegar

Preparation time: 30 minutes

Cooking time: 1 hour 5 minutes

1. Put the chicken in a large bowl or plastic tub and rub in the salt and lime juice. Cover and set aside for 30 minutes.

2. Heat the oil over a medium heat and fry the onions until they are soft but not brown.

3. Add 3 tablespoon water to the ground spice mixture and make a paste. Add this to onions and fry for 2 minutes. Add the garlic and ginger and fry for 2 minutes. Add 2 tablespoons water and cook until the water evaporates.

4. Adjust heat to medium-high and add the chicken. Stir and fry until the chicken changes colour, about 5-6 minutes.

5. Add the warm water and bring to the boil. Cover and simmer for 35-40 minutes.

6. Blend the coconut milk powder with the hot water and add to the chicken. Add the creamed coconut, salt and whole fresh chillies. Stir until the coconut is dissolved. Cover the pan and simmer for 10 minutes

7. Add the vinegar and mix well. Remove from the heat and serve.

Serve with Green Pullao and Cauliflower Ambat.

Suitable for freezing.

BEEF, PORK
AND LAMB

Beef Curry
SERVES 4

*B*eef, a forbidden item in the Hindu religion, is sold and consumed freely in Goa. Here is a land where people belonging to three different religions, Hindu, Muslim and Christian, live in complete harmony and respect each others beliefs and needs.

750g (1¹/₂lb) stewing steak, cut in 2.5cm (1 inch) cubes
60ml (2 fl oz) cider vinegar
60ml (2 fl oz) red wine
8 cloves of garlic, peeled and crushed
3.5cm (1¹/₂ inch) cube of fresh root ginger, peeled and grated
2 bay leaves, crumpled
2 teaspoons coriander seeds
2 teaspoons cummin seeds
Two 5cm (2 inch) pieces cassia bark or cinnamon stick, broken up
4 whole cloves
¹/₄ teaspoon black peppercorns
2-3 dried red chillies, chopped
3 tablespoons sunflower oil
1 large onion, approx 250g (8 oz), finely chopped
1 teaspoon ground turmeric
1 tablespoon tomato purée
600ml (1 pint) warm water
1 teaspoon salt or to taste
75g (2¹/₂ oz) coconut milk powder
125ml (4 fl oz) hot water
125g (4 oz) skinned chopped tomatoes, or canned tomatoes with their juice
2 tablespoons finely chopped fresh coriander leaves

Preparation time: 25 minutes plus marinating
Cooking time: 1 hour 40 minutes

1. Put the meat into a bowl. Mix together the vinegar, wine, ginger, garlic and bay leaves and pour over the meat. Cover and leave in the fridge 4-6 hours. Remove 30 minutes before cooking.
2. Preheat a heavy-based frying pan over a medium heat. Lower the heat and add the coriander, cummin seeds, cassia or cinnamon, cloves, peppercorns and dried chillies, and dry roast them for 2-3 minutes. Stir constantly. Transfer to a plate and cool. When cold, grind in a coffee grinder until fine.
3. Heat the oil over a medium heat and fry the onions until they are just soft, about 5 minutes.
4. Drain the meat and add to the onions. Reserve the marinade. Fry the meat over a high heat for 3-4 minutes, stirring frequently.
5. Add the roasted ground spices and turmeric. Stir and cook for 3-4 minutes or until the liquid evaporates and the sauce is thick and batter-like.
6. Add the marinade, tomato purée and water. Bring to the boil, cover and simmer for 55-60 minutes or until the beef is tender. Mix in the salt.
7. Blend the coconut milk powder with hot water and add to the beef. Cover and simmer for 10 minutes.
8. Add the chopped tomatoes and simmer for 5 minutes. Stir in the coriander leaves and serve.

Serve with Tomato Pullao and Ford.

Suitable for freezing.

Previous pages: Pork Sorpotel and Beef Curry.

Pork Sorpotel

SERVES 4

A well-known Goan delicacy with, perhaps, the strongest Indo-Portuguese flavour. The traditional Sorpotel consists of pork, pig's liver, heart, brain and fresh pig's blood! I offer my version here with only pork and liver.

500g (1 lb) boned shoulder or knuckle end of pork
250g (8 oz) lamb or pig's liver
600ml (1 pint) water
Three 5cm (2 inch) pieces of cassia or cinnamon stick
1 teaspoon whole black peppercorns
6 whole cloves
2.5cm (1 inch) cube unpeeled fresh root ginger, sliced
60ml (2 fl oz) sunflower oil
Mix the following 7 ingredients:
2 teaspoons ground cummin
2 teaspoons ground coriander
1/2-1 teaspoon chilli powder
1 teaspoon ground turmeric
2 teaspoons paprika
1 teaspoon ground cinnamon
1/2 teaspoon ground cloves

5 tablespoons cider vinegar
3 tablespoons water
3.5cm (1 1/2 inch) cube of fresh root ginger, peeled and grated
5 large or 8 small cloves of garlic, peeled and crushed
1 medium onion, approx. 180g (6 oz), finely chopped
2-4 fresh green chillies, seeded and sliced lengthwise
1 teaspoon salt or to taste
250ml (8 fl oz) warm water

Preparation time: 20-25 minutes
Cooking time: 1 hour 10 minutes

1. Put the pork, liver and water in a saucepan over a high heat and bring to the boil. Skim off any scum and add the cassia or cinnamon, peppercorns, cloves and ginger. Reduce the heat to low and cover and simmer for 45 minutes.
2. Lift the meat and liver out with a slotted spoon, and transfer to another dish. Remove any whole spices from the meat. Strain the liquid and reserve.
3. Heat the oil over a medium heat in a large pan and fry the pork and liver until well browned.
4. Mix the ground spices with 3 tablespoons of the vinegar and the water and add to the meat and liver. Reduce the heat to low. Stir and fry for 2 minutes.
5. Add the ginger, garlic, onions, green chillies and salt. Stir and fry for 2-3 minutes over a medium heat. Add half the reserved cooking liquid and cook for 2 minutes. Add the remaining liquid. Stir and cook for a further 2 minutes.
6. Add the warm water. Bring to the boil, cover and simmer for 20 minutes. Stir in the remaining vinegar and remove from the heat.

Serve with the traditional accompaniment of Sanna or with plain rice and Vegetable Stew.

Suitable for freezing.

Pork Assada
SERVES 4

*A*ssada *in Portuguese is roasting or grilling, but in the Indo-Portuguese style, it is often pan roasted. I first tasted this dish in Goa and here offer my version of the recipe.*

750g (1¹/₂ lb) pork shoulder
  steak or spare rib chops,
  trimmed of excess fat
Grind the following 5 ingredi-
ents in a coffee grinder until
fine:
2-6 dried red chillies, chopped
¹/₂ teaspoon cummin seeds
10 black peppercorns
5cm (2 inch) piece of cassia
  bark or cinnamon stick,
  broken up
4 whole cloves

90ml (3 fl oz) cider vinegar
1 teaspoon ground turmeric
1 teaspoon salt or to taste
4 large or 6 small cloves of
  garlic, peeled and chopped
2.5cm (1 inch) cube of fresh
  root ginger, peeled and
  chopped
2 tablespoons sunflower oil
2 medium onions, approx.
  350g (12 oz), finely sliced
2-4 fresh green chillies, seeded
and sliced lengthwise

Preparation time: 25 minutes plus marinating
Cooking time: 1 hour

1. Prick the meat all over with a sharp knife. This will allow flavours to permeate deeper into the meat.
2. Put the ground spices in to a bowl and add the vinegar and turmeric. Mix well.
3. Add the salt to the garlic and ginger and crush to a pulp, using a pestle and mortar or the back of a wooden spoon. Stir this into the vinegar based spice mixture. Put the meat into a large container. Rub the spice paste well into the pork. Cover and leave to marinate in the fridge for 3-4 hours. Remove from the fridge 30 minutes before cooking.
4. Heat the oil over a medium heat in a wide shallow pan. Add the pork and fry for 5-6 minutes. Cover the pan, reduce the heat to low and simmer the pork in its own juice for 45-50 minutes or until the meat is tender.
5. Drain and transfer the pork to a large plate and set aside to cool. Pour off any excess fat from the pan leaving about 4 teaspoons behind. Place the pan over a medium heat and fry the onions and green chillies for 3-4 minutes.
6. Meanwhile, cut the pork into 5mm (¹/₄ inch) thick slices and add to the onion/chilli mixture. Fry for 5-6 minutes stirring frequently and remove from the heat and serve.

Serve with plain boiled rice and Masala Dhal and/or Aubergine Curry

Suitable for freezing.

Pork Assada with Masala Dhal and Chapatties.

Marinated Pork Chops
SERVES 4

I have, again, deviated from the European influence of using vinegar for the marinade. Instead, I have chosen a spice-laced yogurt mixture. The marinated chops are rolled in egg and breadcrumbs and shallow fried; they are truly scrumptious!

4 pork chops, boned shoulder
  or leg steaks can also be used
60g (2 oz) natural yogurt
2.5cm (1 inch) cube of fresh
  root ginger, peeled and
  chopped
2 large cloves of garlic, peeled
  and chopped
1-2 fresh green chillies, seeded
  and chopped
60g (2 oz) chopped onions
15g (^{1}/$_2$ oz) coriander leaves,
including the tender stalks,
  chopped
^{1}/$_2$ teaspoon ground turmeric
^{1}/$_2$ teaspoon ground cinnamon
^{1}/$_2$ teaspoon ground cloves
^{1}/$_2$ teaspoon salt or to taste
Oil for shallow frying
30g (1 oz) plain flour
1 medium egg, beaten
60g (2 oz) fresh breadcrumbs

Preparation time: 15 minutes plus marinating
Cooking time: 20-25 minutes

1. Remove the rind and trim off excess fat from the chops. Beat them with a meat mallet and flatten to about 5mm (^{1}/$_4$ inch) thickness.
2. Put the yogurt, ginger, garlic, green chillies, onions and coriander leaves into a blender or food processor and blend to a smooth purée.
3. Add the turmeric, cinnamon, cloves and salt and blend again.
4. Lay the chops on a large flat dish and spread the puréed ingredients evenly on both sides. Cover and leave to marinate for 3-4 hours or overnight in the fridge. Remove from the fridge 30 minutes before cooking.
5. Pour enough oil into a deep frying pan to cover the base to a depth of 2.5cm (1 inch) and heat over medium to low heat.
6. Dip each pork chop in flour making sure it is fully coated, then dip in beaten egg. Roll in the breadcrumbs and fry gently until they are evenly browned on both sides, about 20-25 minutes. Drain on absorbent paper and serve.

Serve with Cauliflower Pullao or Green Pullao and Carrot Raita.

Suitable for freezing.

Mutton Curry
SERVES 4

Mutton is more easily available in India than lamb. You can, of course, use lamb instead. I have chosen natural yogurt instead of vinegar to marinate the meat.

90g (3 oz) natural yogurt
1 teaspoon ground turmeric
750g (1½ lb) mutton or lamb
  cut into 2.5cm (1 inch) cubes
75ml (2½ fl oz) sunflower
  oil
1 large onion, approx. 250g
  (8 oz), finely sliced
1 large onion, approx. 250g
  (8 oz), finely chopped
3.5cm (1½ inch) cube fresh
  root ginger, peeled and grated
4 large or 6 small cloves of
  garlic, peeled and crushed
1½ tablespoons ground
  coriander
1 teaspoon ground cinnamon
½ teaspoon ground cloves
½ teaspoon freshly milled black
  pepper
½-1 teaspoon chilli powder
2 teaspoons sweet paprika
60g (2 oz) desiccated coconut,
  ground in batches in a coffee
  grinder
375ml (12 fl oz) warm water
1¼ teaspoons salt or to taste
1 tablespoon cider vinegar

Preparation time: 15-20 minutes plus marinating
Cooking time: 1 hour 15 minutes approx.

1. Beat the yogurt and turmeric together. Put the meat in a bowl and add the yogurt. Stir thoroughly. Cover and leave in the fridge to marinate for 3-4 hours or overnight. Remove from the fridge 30 minutes before cooking.

2 Heat half the oil over a medium heat in a heavy based saucepan and fry the sliced onions until browned, about 8-10 minutes. Remove with a slotted spoon, squeezing out as much oil as possible. Drain well.

3. Add the remaining oil to the pan and fry the chopped onions until soft, but not brown. Add the ginger and garlic. Stir and fry for 1 minute.

4. Add the ground coriander, cinnamon, cloves, pepper, chilli powder and paprika. Stir and fry for 1 minute over a low heat. Add 2 tablespoons of water and cook until the water evaporates. Repeat once more. Add the coconut. Stir and fry for 2 minutes over a low heat.

5. Add the meat and adjust the heat to high. Stir and fry the meat for 5 minutes or until it changes colour. Add the water and bring to the boil. Cover the pan and simmer for 30 minutes.

6. Add the fried onions and salt. Re-cover and simmer for a further 30-35 minutes or until the meat is tender.

7. Stir in the vinegar, remove from the heat and serve.

Serve with Garlic Rice and Cauliflower Ambat.

Suitable for freezing.

Pork and Offal Curry
(*Cabidela*)
SERVES 4

I was very curious about how this dish would taste until it was cooked in Goa by an old friend; it tasted superb. Cabidela tastes better 2 days later.

3 cloves of garlic, peeled and
  finely chopped
1/4 teaspoon salt
1/4 teaspoon chilli powder
1/2 teaspoon ground turmeric
60ml (2 fl oz) sunflower oil
500g (1 lb) boned shoulder of
  pork, cut into 2.5cm (1 inch)
  cubes
180g (6 oz) lamb's liver, cut
  into 2.5cm (1 inch) cubes
125g (4 oz) lamb's kidney,
  skinned and cored and cut
  into 2.5cm (1 inch) cubes
Mix the following 5 ingredients:
4 teaspoons ground cummin
1/4 teaspoon freshly milled black
  pepper
1 teaspoon ground cinnamon
1/2 teaspoon ground cloves
1/2 teaspoon ground turmeric

5cm (2 inch) cube of fresh root
  ginger, peeled and chopped
12 cloves of garlic, peeled and
  chopped
1-2 fresh green chillies, seeded
  and chopped
600ml (1 pint) warm water
4 teaspoons tomato purée
1 teaspoon salt or to taste
1 large onion, approx 250g
  (8 oz), finely chopped
2 tablespoons cider vinegar

Preparation time: 30-35 minutes
Cooking time: 45-50 minutes

1. Crush the garlic and salt to a fine paste and add the chilli powder and turmeric.
2. Heat half the oil in a saucepan over a medium heat, and fry the garlic and spice paste for 30 seconds.
3. Add the pork, liver and kidney. Adjust the heat to high and fry for 6-7 minutes or until there is plenty of juice from the meat and offal.
4. Add 3 tablespoons of water to the spice mixture and make a paste. Add the paste to the meat and fry for 6-7 minutes or until all the liquid evaporates.
5. Purée the ginger, garlic and green chillies in a liquidiser or food processor with 60ml (2 fl oz) water and add to the meat. Stir and cook for 6-7 minutes.
6. Add the water, tomato purée and salt. Bring to the boil. Cover and simmer for 20 minutes.
7. Meanwhile, heat the remaining oil over a medium heat and fry the onions until they are a pale golden colour, about 6-8 minutes. Add the onions to the pork and offal. Re-cover and simmer for a further 20 minutes or until the meat and offal are tender.
8. Stir in the vinegar and remove from heat and serve.

Serve with Tomato Pullao or plain boiled rice and Batata Sukke

Suitable for freezing.

Pork and Offal Curry with Batata Sukkhe.

Pork Balchao
SERVES 4

This is an ideal 'do-ahead' dish for it tastes wonderful after 3-4 days and it will keep well in the fridge for about 7 days. Bring it to room temperature and reheat very gently, adding a small amount of warm water if necessary.

75ml (2½ fl oz) sunflower oil
6 cloves of garlic, peeled and crushed
2.5cm (1 inch) cube of fresh root ginger, peeled and grated
Grind the following 5 ingredients in a coffee grinder until fine:
Two 2.5cm (1 inch) pieces cassia bark or cinnamon sticks, broken up
2 dried red chillies, chopped
4 whole cloves
2 teaspoons cummin seeds
10 black peppercorns

750g (1½ lb) pork loin or shoulder steak, cut into 2.5cm (1 inch) cubes
1 teaspoon ground turmeric
200ml (7 fl oz) warm water
1½ tablespoons tomato purée
¼ teaspoon chilli powder, optional
1 large onion, approx. 250g (8 oz) finely sliced
4 cloves garlic, peeled and crushed
2.5cm (1 inch) cube of fresh root ginger, peeled and finely grated
1 teaspoon salt or to taste
1 tablespoon cider vinegar

Preparation time: 25 minutes
Cooking time: 1 hour 15 minutes

1. Heat half the oil in a heavy-sbased saucepan over a medium heat.
2. Add the garlic and ginger and fry for 30 seconds.
3. Add the ground spices and fry for 30 seconds.
4. Add the pork and turmeric and fry for 5 minutes or until the meat starts to release its juices.
5. Add the water, tomato purée and chilli powder, if used. Bring to the boil, cover and simmer for 35 minutes.
6. Meanwhile, heat the remaining oil in a small saucepan over a medium heat and fry the onions until they are a pale golden colour.
7. Add the garlic and ginger and fry for 2-3 minutes, stirring constantly.
8. Add the mixture to the pork. Cover and simmer for 30-35 minutes or until pork is tender.
9. Stir in the salt and vinegar and remove from the heat and serve.

Serve with Sanna or plain boiled rice, Brinjal Pickle and Masala Dhal.

Suitable for freezing.

Meat Loaf
SERVES 4

A meat loaf in the Indo-Portuguese style is a totally unique taste. Thick, juicy slices, packed with wonderful flavours, it is ideal for a family meal and is an excellent choice for picnics and buffet parties. You can give any leftover meat loaf a new taste by frying the slices in a little hot oil until they are evenly browned on both sides.

2 large slices of white bread, about 125g (4 oz)

500g (1 lb) minced mutton, lamb or beef

1 small onion, approx. 125g (4 oz), chopped

2 large cloves of garlic, peeled and coarsely chopped

2.5cm (1 inch) cube fresh root ginger, peeled and coarsely chopped

1-2 fresh green chillies, seeded and chopped

15g (½ oz) fresh coriander leaves including the tender stalks, chopped

2 tablespoons fresh chopped mint or 2 teaspoons mint chutney

1 tablespoon ground coriander

2 teaspoons ground cummin

½-1 teaspoon chilli powder

1 teaspoon garam masala

1 teaspoon salt or to taste

1 medium egg

30g (1 oz) desiccated coconut, ground in a coffee grinder until fine

crisp lettuce leaves for serving

Preparation time: 15 minutes
Cooking time: 1 hour

1. Preheat the oven to 200°C, 400°F, Gas Mark 6.
2. Soak the bread in cold water for 5 minutes and then squeeze out all the water.
3. Put all the ingredients, except the lettuce leaves, in a food processor and blend until the mixture is smooth.
4. Lightly grease a 900g (2 lb) loaf tin and pack the meat mixture into it.
5. Bake in the centre of the oven for 1 hour.
6. Remove from the oven and allow to stand for 10 minutes. Pour off any liquid and turn the meat loaf out onto a plate.
7. Serve surrounded with crisp lettuce leaves.

Serve hot with boiled new potatoes or cold with a mixed salad.

Suitable for freezing.

Mixed Meat Stew
SERVES 4

Goan food is a perfect example of the harmonious blend of different religions. Beef and pork are sold and consumed freely by the majority of Christians in Goa, while Muslims are forbidden to eat pork and Hindus will not eat beef.

180g (6 oz) trimmed, lean
stewing beef

180g (6 oz) boned and trimmed
lean pork, shoulder or leg

180g (6 oz) skinned and boned
chicken thighs

180g (6 oz) spicy Goan
sausages (see page 81) or any
other fresh spicy sausages

125ml (4 fl oz) water

75ml (2½ fl oz) sunflower oil

1 large onion, approx. 250g
(8 oz), finely sliced

4 large cloves of garlic, peeled
and crushed

3.5cm (1½ inch) cube of fresh
root ginger, peeled and grated

1 teaspoon ground turmeric

450ml (¾ pint) warm Goan
stock (see page 20) or water

6 whole cloves

Two 5cm (2 inch) pieces of
cassia bark or cinnamon
stick, halved

180g (6 oz) potatoes, peeled
and cut into 2.5cm (1 inch)
cubes

1 teaspoon ground cummin

150ml (5 fl oz) single cream

1 teaspoon salt or to taste

½ teaspoon freshly milled black
pepper

Preparation time: 25-30 minutes
Cooking time: 60 minutes

1. Cut the beef, pork and chicken into 2.5cm (1 inch) cubes.

2. Grill the sausages until well browned. Cool and cut each sausage into 3-4 pieces.

3. Put the beef in a saucepan and add the 125ml (4 fl oz) water and bring to the boil over a high heat. Reduce the heat to medium, cover the pan and cook for 15-20 minutes or until the beef is completely dry.

4. Heat the oil over a medium heat in a heavy-based saucepan and fry the onions until they are soft but not brown.

5. Add the boiled beef, pork, garlic, ginger and turmeric. Stir and fry for 3-4 minutes.

6. Add the stock or water, cloves and cassia or cinnamon. Cover the pan and simmer for 20 minutes.

7. Add the chicken and bring back to the boil. Cover and simmer for 10 minutes.

8. Add the potatoes, sausages and cummin. Cover and simmer for 20-25 minutes or until the potatoes are tender.

9. Add the cream, salt and pepper, stir and mix well. Simmer uncovered for 5-6 minutes, remove from the heat and serve.

Serve with Garlic Rice and Ford.

Suitable for freezing. Freeze without potatoes and add cooked potatoes when reheating.

Mixed Meat Stew with Ford.

Meat Chilli Fry

SERVES 4

*T*his is a fairly easy dish to prepare although it involves a two-stage cooking process. The first stage can be done 3-4 days in advance and stored in the fridge.

750g (1½ lb) boned leg of lamb
  or stewing steak
90ml (3 fl oz) cider vinegar
1 medium onion, approx. 150g
  (5 oz), finely chopped
1 teaspoon ground turmeric
1-2 long slim dried red chillies,
  chopped
6 whole cloves
180ml (6 fl oz) water
2 tablespoons sunflower oil
1 large onion, approx. 250g
  (8 oz), finely sliced
6 cloves of garlic, peeled and
  crushed
3.5cm (1½ inch) cube of
  fresh root ginger, peeled and
  grated
250g (8 oz) chopped canned
  tomatoes with their juice
1 tablespoon ground cummin
½-1 teaspoon chilli powder
1 teaspoon garam masala
45g (1½ oz) creamed coconut,
  cut into small pieces
15g (½ oz) fresh coriander
  leaves, including the tender
  stalks, chopped
1 tablespoon fresh chopped
  mint or 1 teaspoon mint
  sauce or mint chutney
4 whole fresh green chillies

Preparation time: 15-20 minutes
Cooking time: 2-2½ hours

1. Cut the meat into 2.5cm (1 inch) cubes and add the vinegar, onions, turmeric, red chillies and cloves. Mix thoroughly, cover the container and leave to marinate in the fridge for 4-6 hours. Remove from the fridge 30 minutes before cooking.
2. Put the meat and marinade into a saucepan and add the water. Bring to the boil, cover and simmer until the meat is tender, about 1½-2 hours. At this stage you can cool and refrigerate the meat and finish cooking the day you want to serve it.
3. Heat the oil over a medium heat and fry the onions until they are soft but not brown. Add the garlic and ginger and fry for 1 minute. Add the tomatoes. Stir and cook for 2-3 minutes. Add the cummin and chilli powder. Stir and cook for 1 minute.
4. Drain the cooked meat, with the chillies and cloves, and add to the tomato spice mixture. Reserve the cooking liquid. Stir and fry the meat over medium to high heat for 4-5 minutes. Add the garam masala and fry for 1 minute.
5. Heat the reserved liquid. Add the creamed coconut, stir until it has dissolved, then add to the meat. Cook over a medium heat for 2-3 minutes.
6. Add the coriander leaves, mint and whole chillies. Cook for 2-3 minutes stirring constantly. Remove from the heat and serve.

Serve with Chapatties and/or Garlic Rice and Aubergine Curry or Vegetable Stew.

Suitable for freezing.

Pork Vindaloo
SERVES 4

Vindaloo needs little or no introduction: ask anybody who has fancied a curry after a drinks party! Yes, it is a hot dish, but when cooked correctly, the chillies blend perfectly with other spices allowing you to enjoy all the flavours.

625g (1¹/₄ lb) boned leg or
  shoulder of pork
1 quantity of Marinade
  (see page 80)
4 tablespoons sunflower oil
1 large onion, approx. 250g
  (8oz), finely chopped
5cm (2 inch) piece cassia bark
  or cinnamon stick, halved
*Grind the following 8
ingredients until fine:*
4 whole green cardamom pods
4 whole cloves
¹/₂ a whole nutmeg, lightly
  crushed
1 teaspoon cummin seeds
1 tablespoon coriander seeds
1 teaspoon fenugreek seeds
¹/₂ teaspoon black peppercorns
2 bay leaves, cut into pieces

¹/₄-¹/₂ teaspoon chilli powder
1 teaspoon sweet paprika
1 tablespoon tomato purée
250ml (8 fl oz) warm water
250g (8 oz) potatoes, peeled
  and cut into 2.5cm (1 inch)
  cubes
1¹/₂ teaspoons salt or to taste
2 teaspoons light brown sugar
4 whole fresh green chillies
2 tablespoons chopped fresh
  coriander leaves

Preparation time: 30 minutes plus marinating
Cooking time: 1 hour 40 minutes

1. Trim off any excess fat from the meat. Cut the meat into 2.5cm (1 inch) cubes and put into a container. Add the marinade, stir and mix thoroughly. Cover the container and leave to marinate for 4-6 hours or overnight in the fridge. Remove from the fridge 30 minutes before cooking.

2. Heat the oil over a medium heat and fry the onions and cassia or cinnamon until the onions are soft but not brown.

3. Add the ground ingredients and fry for 1 minute. Add 1 tablespoon water and fry for a further minute. Repeat this process twice more.

4. Lift out the marinated meat with a slotted spoon and add to the pan. Reserve any remaining marinade. Adjust the heat to high and fry the meat for 5-6 minutes, stirring continuously.

5. Add the chilli powder, paprika, tomato purée and the reserved marinade. Mix well. Add the warm water, bring to the boil, cover and simmer for 45-50 minutes.

6. Add the potatoes, salt and sugar. Bring to the boil again, re-cover and simmer for 15-20 minutes or until the potatoes are tender.

7. Add the whole fresh chillies and coriander leaves and simmer uncovered for 3-4 minutes.

Serve with plain boiled rice and Masala Dhal

Suitable for freezing. Freeze without the potatoes and add cooked potatoes when reheating the dish.

Roast Lamb
SERVES 4

A fine example of Eastern flavour and Western cooking method, this dish which is marinated for 3-4 days, will make a wonderful centrepiece for your dinner party.

1.25kg (2¹/₂ lb) leg of lamb, trimmed of excess fat
1 quantity of Marinade, (see page 80)
30g (1 oz) ghee or 15g (¹/₂ oz) unsalted butter
4 tablespoons sunflower oil
1 small onion, approx. 125g (4 oz), very finely chopped
2 cloves garlic, peeled and crushed
1cm (¹/₂ inch) cube of fresh root ginger, peeled and finely grated
¹/₄-¹/₂ teaspoon chilli powder
¹/₄ teaspoon ground turmeric
1 teaspoon ground coriander
¹/₂ teaspoon ground cummin
125g (4 oz) tomatoes, skinned and chopped or canned tomatoes with juice
1 tablespoon tomato purée
2 tablespoons finely chopped fresh coriander leaves
sprigs of fresh coriander leaves

Preparation time: 25 minutes plus marinating
Cooking time: 2 hours

1. Using a sharp knife, make several deep incisions all over the lamb. Put the lamb in a bowl, pour on the marinade and rub well into the meat.
2. Cover the bowl tightly and leave in the fridge for 36-48 hours. Turn the meat over at least once a day. Remove from the fridge 1 hour before cooking.
3. Preheat the oven to 200°C, 400°F, Gas Mark 6.
4. Heat the ghee or butter and 2 tablespoons oil over a medium heat in a frying pan. Lift out the meat from the marinade and brown all over in hot fat. Reserve any marinade.
5. Place the meat in a roasting tin and pour over any reserved marinade. Cover very loosely with foil. Cook in the centre of the oven for 35-40 minutes.
6. Reduce the temperature to 160°C, 325°F, Gas Mark 3, and cook for 1 hour 10 minutes. Remove and set aside. Strain the cooking liquid into a jug and drain off all the fat.
7. Heat the remaining oil over a medium heat and fry the onion until soft. Add the garlic and ginger and fry for 1 minute. Add the chilli powder, turmeric, coriander and cummin. Stir and fry for 1 minute.
8. Add the tomatoes, tomato purée and strained meat juices. Cook gently, stirring, until the sauce is paste-like. Stir in the fresh coriander leaves. Remove from the heat. Cut lamb into slices, spoon over sauce and garnish with fresh coriander.

Serve with Tomato Pullao and Ford.

Suitable for freezing.

Roast Lamb with Tomato Pullao.

Marinade for Pork Vindaloo

150ml (5 fl oz) cider vinegar
2 long slim dried red chillies,
  chopped
30g (1 oz) fresh root ginger,
  peeled and coarsely chopped
30g (1 oz) cloves of garlic,
  peeled and coarsely chopped
1 teaspoon ground turmeric

1. Place the vinegar in a blender or food processor and add the red chillies, ginger and garlic and blend until very smooth. If you do not have a blender or food processor, pound them with pestle and mortar and mix with the vinegar. Add the ground turmeric to the blended ingredients and use as required for Pork Vindaloo, (see page 77).

Marinade for Roast Lamb.

1 medium onion, approx. 180g
  (6 oz)
4 cloves garlic
2.5cm (1 inch) cube of fresh
  root ginger
125ml (4 fl oz) dry white wine
2 teaspoons ground coriander
1 teaspoon ground cummin
$^1/_2$ teaspoon chilli powder
$^1/_2$ teaspoon ground cloves
$^1/_4$ teaspoon ground cinnamon
$^1/_4$ teaspoon freshly milled black
  pepper
$^1/_2$ teaspoon salt or to taste

1. Peel and coarsely chop the onion. Peel and chop the garlic and ginger.
2. Put the onion, garlic, ginger and wine into a blender or food processor, and blend to a smooth purée.
3. Transfer the purée to a mixing bowl and add the coriander, cummin, chilli powder, cloves, cinnamon, pepper and salt. Mix well. Use as required for Roast Lamb, (see page 78).

Goan Sausages
MAKES 24 SAUSAGES

These spicy Goan sausages are traditionally laced with 'Feni', a Goan spirit, of which there are two varieties, made from the coconut palm and the cashew palm. I have made these sausages using Gin instead, and they are delicious. If you cannot obtain sausage casings then simply roll the mixture into sausage shapes, dust with flour and grill or fry.

1-2 long slim, dried red chillies, chopped
¹/₂ teaspoon cummin seeds
¹/₂ teaspoon coriander seeds
6 black peppercorns
3 whole cloves
2.5cm (1 inch) piece of cassia bark or cinnamon stick, broken up
180ml (6 fl oz) cider vinegar
10-12 large cloves of garlic, peeled and chopped
5cm (2 inch) cube of fresh root ginger, peeled and chopped
1-2 fresh green chillies, seeded and chopped
90ml (3 fl oz) dry gin
900g (2 lb) pork sausage meat
1 teaspoon salt or to taste
sausage casing

Preparation time: 1¹/₂ hours
Cooking time: 10 minutes

1. Preheat a small heavy-based frying pan over a medium heat. Add the chillies, cummin, coriander, peppercorns, cloves and cassia or cinnamon. Reduce heat to low and roast the spices gently until they release their aroma, about 1-2 minutes. Put the spices on a plate and allow them to cool. Grind in a coffee grinder until fine.
2. Place the vinegar, garlic, ginger and green chillies in a blender or food processor and purée until very smooth. Add the ground spices and gin to the blender and process until thoroughly mixed.
3. Put the sausagemeat and salt into a large mixing bowl and add the spice mixture. Mix thoroughly until all the ingredients are blended together.
4. Using a piping bag with a large nozzle, fill the sausage casings with the mixture. Twist and tie at 7.5cm-10cm (3-4 inch) intervals.
5. Boil the sausages in a large pan of boiling water, for about 10 minutes, then drain and soak them in cold water. When cold, freeze or refrigerate and use as required.
6. To cook, fry or grill them in their own fat until golden brown.

Serve with Tomato Pullao and Vegetable Stew or boiled new potatoes and Broccoli Upkari.

Suitable for freezing.

RICE AND BREADS

Prawn Pullao

SERVES 4

Spiced prawns, combined with delicately flavoured Basmati rice, is sure to be a hot favourite with prawn lovers and Pullao or 'Pilau Rice' fans.

250g (8 oz) Basmati rice, washed and soaked in cold water for 30 minutes

45g (1½ oz) ghee or unsalted butter

1 teaspoon caraway seeds

Two 5cm (2 inch) pieces cassia bark or cinnamon stick

4 whole cloves

4 green cardamoms split at the top of each pod

10 black peppercorns

2 bay leaves, crumpled

1 medium onion, approx. 150g (5 oz), finely sliced

½ teaspoon salt or to taste

500ml (16 fl oz) warm water

1 quantity Spiced Prawns, (see opposite)

Preparation time: 20-25 minutes
Cooking time: 25-30 minutes

1. Drain the rice and set aside.
2. Melt the ghee or butter in a heavy based saucepan over a medium heat. Add the caraway seeds and fry for 30 seconds. Add the cassia or cinnamon, cloves, cardamoms, peppercorns and bay leaves. Let the spices sizzle for 30 seconds.
3. Add the onions and fry until they are a pale golden colour, about 8-9 minutes.
4. Add the drained rice. Stir and fry for 2-3 minutes.
5. Add the salt and water. Bring to the boil, cover the pan tightly and reduce the heat to very low. Cook for 10 minutes without lifting the lid.
6. Remove from the heat and leave undisturbed for 10 minutes.
7. Transfer the rice to a very large dish and add the hot spiced prawns. Gently fork through to mix well. The Pullao can be reheated in the microwave if necessary.

Serve the traditional way with a Raita, Pappodum and a dry item such as a cutlet. If you prefer a dish with a sauce then serve with Cauliflower Ambat or Vegetable Stew.

Suitable for freezing if fresh prawns are used.

Previous pages: Goan Poori, Prawn Pullao, Rice Chapatties and Sanna.

Spiced Prawns for Prawn Pullao.

You can cook the prawns in advance and store in the fridge for up to 48 hours. The spices and the vinegar will act as excellent preservatives.

2 tablespoons ghee or unsalted
  butter
1 medium onion, approx. 150g
  (5 oz), finely sliced
1-2 fresh green chillies, seeded
  and sliced lengthwise
6 cloves garlic, peeled and
  crushed
2.5cm (1 inch) cube of fresh
  root ginger, peeled and finely
  grated
2 teaspoons ground coriander
1 teaspoons ground cummin
$\frac{1}{2}$ teaspoon ground cinnamon
$\frac{1}{2}$ teaspoon ground cardamom
$\frac{1}{2}$ teaspoon ground turmeric
125g (4 oz) chopped canned
  tomatoes and their juice
30g (1 oz) creamed coconut,
  cut into small pieces
400g (14 oz) peeled fresh
  cooked prawns, or frozen
  prawns thawed, drained and
  dried
$\frac{1}{2}$ teaspoon salt or to taste
2 tablespoons chopped fresh
  coriander leaves
1 tablespoon cider vinegar

1. Melt the ghee or butter in a heavy based saucepan over a medium heat. Add the onions, fresh chillies, garlic and ginger. Stir and fry until they are soft but not brown.
2. Add the coriander, cummin, cinnamon and cardamom. Stir and fry for 1 minute. Stir in the turmeric and half the tomatoes. Stir and cook until the tomato juice evaporates. Add the remaining tomatoes. Stir and cook until the spice mixture is dry again.
3. Add the coconut and stir until dissolved.
4. Add the prawns, salt and coriander leaves. Stir and cook for 2-3 minutes.
5. Stir in the vinegar and remove from the heat. Use as required for Prawn Pullao, (see opposite).

Portuguese Pullao
(*Arroz Refogado*)
SERVES 4

In Portuguese, 'Arroz' means rice; 'Refogado' is the preparation of onions and other spices by 'sweating' them before the rice is added. A good stock is essential for this recipe so use the stock for Caldo Verde (see page 20) or buy good quality fresh stock from supermarkets.

250g (8 oz) Basmati rice, washed and soaked for 30 minutes and drained

2 hard boiled eggs

4 Goan Sausages, (see page 81) or any fresh spicy sausage

45g (1½ oz) ghee or unsalted butter

4 whole cloves

Two 5cm (2 inch) pieces cassia bark or cinnamon sticks, halved

4 green cardamoms, split

10 black peppercorns

2.5cm (1 inch) cube of fresh root ginger, peeled and cut into julienne sticks

4 large cloves of garlic, peeled and sliced

1 large onion, approx. 250g (8 oz), finely sliced

1-2 fresh green chillies, seeded and sliced lengthwise

¼ teaspoon ground turmeric

500ml (16 fl oz) Goan stock, (see page 20) or chicken stock

¼ teaspoon salt or to taste

2 tablespoons finely chopped fresh coriander leaves

Preparation time: 30 minutes
Cooking time: 25 minutes

1. Shell the eggs and quarter them lengthwise and set aside.

2. Skin the sausages and fry gently in their own fat until well browned. When cool enough to handle, cut each sausage diagonally into 3-4 thick slices.

3. Melt the ghee or butter gently over a medium to low heat and add the cloves, cassia or cinnamon, cardamoms, black pepper, ginger and garlic. Stir and fry for 1 minute.

4. Add the onions and fresh chillies. Stir and fry for 2-3 minutes. Cover the pan and reduce the heat to low. Let the onions sweat for 5 minutes. Remove the lid and stir the onions once. Re-cover and cook for a further 2-3 minutes.

5. Add the turmeric and rice. Stir and fry for 2-3 minutes. Add the stock, salt and coriander leaves. Stir once and bring to the boil. Cover the pan tightly and reduce the heat to very low. Cook, covered, for 10 minutes.

6. Remove from the heat and leave undisturbed for 10 minutes. Fork through the rice and turn onto a serving dish. Arrange the sausages and eggs on top.

Serve with Aubergine Curry or Cauliflower Ambat accompanied by Cucumber Raita.

Suitable for freezing without the sausages and eggs.

Portuguese Pullao.

Rice Chapatti
(Apa De Arroz)
MAKES 8

These are totally different from the traditional wheat flour Chapatties and are good enough to eat on their own! They are truly delicious and are one of those things which you can easily over-eat without realising!

50g (5 oz) ground rice
75g (2¹/₂ oz) plain flour
45g (1¹/₂ oz) desiccated
   coconut, ground in a coffee
   grinder until fine
1-2 fresh green chillies, seeded
   and chopped
3 tablespoons finely chopped
   fresh coriander leaves
¹/₂ teaspoon salt or to taste
300ml (¹/₂ pint) water
Oil for shallow frying

Preparation time: 10 minutes
Cooking time: 40-45 minutes

1. Put all the ingredients, except the water and oil, into a mixing bowl and mix well.
2. Gradually add the water and mix until a thick batter is formed. This should be of spreading consistency.
3. Heat 2 teaspoons oil in a heavy-based frying pan, preferably non-stick, over a medium heat.
4. Spread 2 tablespoons batter in the base of the pan to form a disc which should be approximately 15cm (6 inches) in diameter. Cook for 3-4 minutes or until the underside has brown patches and the top is well set.
5. Spread a little oil on the top of the Chapatti and then turn it over. Cook for a further 2-3 minutes or until brown.
6. Line a large tray with absorbent paper and arrange the cooked chapatties in a single layer on top. If you stack them up, the bottom ones will turn soggy. They can be reheated briefly under a low grill.

Serve with Prawn Balchao, Brinjal Pickle etc. or Fried Chilli Chicken.

Unsuitable for freezing.

Goan Poori
(Vodde)
MAKES 24

*P*oori *is a very popular bread all over India. It is an unleavened bread which is deep fried and served with any meat, poultry or vegetable dish with little or no sauce. Pooris are difficult to reheat, so you will need to fry them just before serving. They are finger licking good!*

250g (8 oz) Chapatti flour
60g (2 oz) fine semolina
$^1/_2$ teaspoon salt
$^1/_2$ teaspoon sugar
30g (1 oz) butter
150ml (5 fl oz) warm water
Oil for deep frying

Preparation time: 30 minutes
Cooking time: 20-25 minutes

1. Put the flour, semolina, salt and sugar into a bowl and mix well. Rub in the butter.
2. Gradually add the water and knead until a stiff dough is formed. Add a little more or less water, as necessary.
3. Knead the dough for 5 minutes then cover with a damp cloth or put into a large plastic food bag. Leave the dough to rest for at least 30 minutes.
4. Divide the dough in half and form into 2 round cakes. Dust with a little flour and roll each one out to about 26cm ($10^1/_2$ inches) in diameter. Using a 6.5cm ($3^1/_2$ inch) cutter, cut out 24 small discs.
5. Heat the oil over a medium heat in a small saucepan, wok, or deep fat fryer. Heat the oil to 160°C (325°F). If you do not have a fat thermometer, drop a tiny piece of dough into the oil. If it floats at once without browning then the oil is ready.
6. Place a Poori in the hot oil and using a flat perforated spoon, gently press it down and let go immediately. When the Poori puffs up, let it brown on the underside. When it is brown, turn it over and brown the other side. Drain on absorbent paper.

Serve with Fried Chilli Chicken, Batata Sukkhe, Meat Chilli Fry etc.

Unsuitable for freezing.

Green Pullao
SERVES 4

*A*n unusual and excellent dish for any occasion, this is a perfect example of the *'Saraswat' community's culinary skills in turning the simple to the sublime!*

250g (8 oz) Basmati rice, washed and soaked in cold water for 30 minutes

30g (1 oz) desiccated coconut

150ml (5 fl oz) hot water

4 cloves garlic, peeled and chopped

2.5cm (1 inch) cube of fresh root ginger, peeled and chopped

15g (½ oz) fresh coriander leaves including the tender stalks

1-2 fresh green chillies, seeded and chopped

60g (2 oz) ghee or unsalted butter

1 teaspoon caraway seeds

Two 5cm (2 inch) pieces cassia bark or cinnamon stick, halved

4 whole cloves

10 black peppercorns

30g (1 oz) unroasted shelled cashews, split

1 large onion, approx. 250g (8 oz), finely sliced

75g (2½ oz) whole green beans, cut into 2.5cm (1 inch) pieces

75g (2½ oz) frozen peas, thawed, or fresh cooked peas

1 teaspoon salt or to taste

500ml (16 fl oz) warm water

1½ tablespoons lime juice

Preparation time: 30 minutes
Cooking time: 25 minutes

1. Drain the rice and set aside.
2. Soak the coconut in hot water for 10 minutes. Put the coconut and water into a blender or food processor and add the garlic, ginger, fresh coriander and fresh chillies. Purée until very smooth.
3. Heat the ghee or butter over a low heat and add the caraway seeds, cassia or cinnamon, cloves, peppercorns and cashews. Let the spices sizzle gently for 1 minute.
4. Add the onions and fry over a medium heat until they are a pale golden colour, about 8-9 minutes.
5. Add the drained rice. Stir and fry for 2-3 minutes. Add the coconut mixture. Stir and fry for 2-3 minutes.
6. Add the beans, peas, salt and water. Bring to the boil, cover the pan tightly and reduce the heat to very low. Cook for 10 minutes without lifting the lid. Remove from the heat and set aside for 10 minutes.
7. Add the lime juice and mix gently with a fork or flat plastic spoon. Wooden spoons or other thick spoons will squash the grains.

Serve with Broccoli Pakode, Batata Cutlets and Carrot or Cucumber Raita, for an excellent and satisfying vegetarian meal. Or serve with Prawn Cutlets, Fish cakes, Marinated Pork Chops etc.

Suitable for freezing.

Green Pullao.

Sanna

MAKES 14 SANNAS

Sanna is a festive Goan bread which is usually made at Easter. Rice is soaked overnight, then ground and allowed to ferment. To aid fermentation, Goans use "Toddy", (see glossary page 13) but I have adapted the recipe to use ground rice and easy blend yeast.

75g (2¹/₂ oz) desiccated
   coconut, ground in a coffee
   grinder until fine
180ml (6 fl oz) hot water
300g (10 oz) ground rice
2¹/₂ teaspoons easy blend yeast
1 teaspoon sugar
1 teaspoon salt
300ml (¹/₂ pint) lukewarm
water

Preparation time: 10-15 minutes, plus time for proving
Cooking time : 10-12 minutes

1. Soak the coconut in the hot water and leave to cool to lukewarm. This is important as the yeast will not activate if the temperature is too high or too low.
2. In a large bowl, mix together the ground rice, yeast, sugar and salt. Gradually add the lukewarm water and mix with a wooden spoon until a thick batter is formed.
3. Stir in the soaked coconut along with any liquid. Cover the bowl and leave in a warm place for an hour.
4. To cook in a steamer or pressure cooker, put 1 heaped tablespoon of the prepared batter into 6-8 small well-greased bowls or ramekins. Steam for 10-12 minutes. If using a pressure cooker, steam without the weight.
5. To cook in a 650 watt microwave; put 1 heaped tablespoon of the prepared batter into 4 well-greased small bowls or ramekins. Cover with microfilm and puncture or peel back slightly. Cook on HIGH for 3 minutes then on MEDIUM for a further 1 minute. Stand for 2 minutes. Turn out and serve.
Adjust timings as necessary if your microwave has a different output.

Serve the Sannas with any meat dish.

Suitable for freezing.

Chapatties
MAKES 8

Chapatties are made from a special type of wholewheat flour. It is sold under the brand names 'Chapatti Flour' or 'Atta' by Indian grocers.

350g (12 oz) Chapatti flour
$1/2$ teaspoon sugar
$1/2$ teaspoon salt
75ml ($2^1/2$ fl oz) vegetable or
corn oil
180ml (6 fl oz) warm water
A little extra flour for dusting
30g (1 oz) butter, melted

Preparation time: 15 minutes plus resting the dough
Cooking time: 25-30 minutes

1. Put the flour in a bowl and mix in the sugar and salt. Add half the oil and rub in until the flour resembles coarse breadcrumbs.
2. Gradually add the water and knead until a soft dough is formed. Add the remaining oil and knead for about 2 minutes.
3. Transfer the dough to a pastry board and knead until smooth and pliable, about 5 minutes.
4. Put the dough in a bowl and cover with a damp cloth. Leave to rest for 30 minutes.
5. Divide the dough into 8 equal portions. Roll each portion between your palms to form a smooth ball and flatten by pressing it down.
6. Preheat a heavy-based frying pan or griddle over a medium to high heat. Roll a flattened cake into a 20cm (8 inch) disc. Keep the rest covered while you are working on one. Place the rolled out Chapatti on the griddle and roll out the next one.
7. Cook the Chapatti for 2 minutes and turn it over with a thin spatula. Cook for 2-3 minutes or until brown spots appear on the underside. Turn the Chapatti over again and cook until brown spots appear on the other side.
8. Line a large plate with absorbent paper. Place the cooked Chapatti on the plate and brush generously with melted butter. Cook the rest of the Chapatties the same way and pile on top of one another.

Serve with Beef Curry, Chilli Chicken etc.

Suitable for freezing.

Cauliflower Pullao
SERVES 4

This dish is in a class of its own. Rice and cauliflower are cooked in coconut milk which is flavoured with a mixture of whole and ground spices; the result is totally irresistible! Traditionally, only cauliflower is added to the rice, but I have included a little sweetcorn and garden peas for added colour.

250g (8 oz) Basmati rice, washed and soaked for 30 minutes

1 cauliflower, approx. 400g (14 oz) when outer leaves are removed

60g (2 oz) ghee or unsalted butter

6 green cardamoms, split at the top of each pod

6 whole cloves

Two 5cm (2 inch) pieces cassia bark or cinnamon stick, halved

1 large onion, approx. 250g (8 oz), finely sliced

4 teaspoons ground coriander

1 teaspoon ground cinnamon

$1/2$ teaspoon ground cloves

$1/4$ -$1/2$ teaspoon chilli powder

60g (2 oz) frozen garden peas, thawed

60g (2 oz) frozen sweetcorn, thawed

$1^{1}/4$ teaspoons salt or to taste

45g ($1^{1}/2$ oz) coconut milk powder

500ml (16 fl oz) warm water

15g ($1/2$ oz) chopped fresh coriander leaves

Preparation time: 20 minutes plus soaking
Cooking time: 20 minutes

1. Drain the rice and set aside.
2. Cut the cauliflower into 3.5cm ($1^{1}/2$ inch) florets.
3. Heat the ghee or butter in a heavy-based pan over a medium heat.
4. Add the cardamoms, cloves and cassia or cinnamon. Let the spices sizzle for 30 seconds.
5. Add the onions and fry until they are a pale golden colour. Stir frequently.
6. Add the ground coriander and fry for 1 minute.
7. Add the cinnamon, cloves and chilli powder and fry for 30 seconds.
8. Add drained rice, cauliflower, peas, sweetcorn and salt. Stir and fry for 2-3 minutes.
9. Blend the coconut milk powder with warm water and add to the rice. Bring to the boil. Cover the pan tightly and reduce heat to very low. Cook for 10 minutes without lifting the lid. Remove from the heat and leave the pan undisturbed for 10 minutes.
10. Fork through the rice and using a metal or plastic spoon transfer it to a serving dish. Garnish with the chopped coriander leaves.

Serve with Masala Dhal and Prawn Cutlets, or Batata Cutlets and a Raita for a vegetarian meal.

Suitable for freezing.

Cauliflower Pullao.

Tomato Pullao
SERVES 4

The Goans practically live off their land. As with most low-lying coastal areas with heavy rainfall, rice is grown extensively. Goan cuisine indulges in wonderful rice dishes which are served with equally wonderful fish and other seafood found along Goa's luxuriant coastline.

250g (8 oz) Basmati or other long grain rice, washed and soaked in cold water for 30 minutes
45g (1½ oz) ghee or unsalted butter
4 green cardamoms, split at the top of each pod
4 cloves
10 whole black peppercorns
Two 5cm (2 inch) pieces cassia bark or cinnamon stick, halved
1 large onion, preferably red, approx. 250g (8 oz), finely sliced
180g (6 oz) chopped canned tomatoes, sieved
375ml (12 fl oz) warm water
½ teaspoon salt or to taste
1 tablespoon chopped fresh coriander leaves

Preparation time: 10-15 minutes plus soaking
Cooking time: 15-20 minutes

1. Drain the rice and set aside.
2. Melt the ghee or butter gently over a medium to low heat and add the cardamom, cloves, black pepper and cinnamon or cassia. Let the spices sizzle gently for about 30 seconds.
3. Add the onions. Stir and fry until they just begin to brown, about 6-8 minutes. Add the drained rice. Stir and fry for 2-3 minutes.
4. Mix the sieved tomatoes and water together. Make sure the total quantity is 500ml (16 fl oz) for Basmati rice and 560ml (18 fl oz) for other long grain rice. If you have less than this, make up the quantity by adding extra water.
5. Add the tomato/water mixture to the rice. Bring to the boil and add the salt. Allow to boil for 1 minute. Cover the pan tightly and reduce heat to very low and cook, 10 minutes for Basmati rice, 12-15 minutes for other long grain rice. Do not lift the lid during cooking as this results in loss of steam which is vital to successful rice cooking. Remove the pan from the heat and leave undisturbed for 10 minutes.
6. Fork through the rice and serve garnished with chopped coriander leaves.

Serve with Jhinga Caldeen, Chicken Cafreal etc. accompanied by Batata Sukkhe.

Suitable for freezing.

Garlic Rice
SERVES 4

*G*oans generally prefer plain boiled rice. Their superbly flavoured dishes go better with rice that has very little added flavour. However, rice flavoured with one or two spices can also make a perfect accompaniment to some Goan dishes. Garlic Rice is an excellent example.

250g (8 oz) Basmati rice
2 tablespoons sunflower oil
¹/₂ teaspoon cummin seeds
4 large cloves of garlic, peeled
  and finely sliced
¹/₂ teaspoon salt or to taste
500ml (16 fl oz) warm water
fresh coriander sprigs to
  garnish

Preparation time: 10 minutes plus soaking
Cooking time: 12-14 minutes

1. Wash the rice and soak in cold water for 30 minutes then drain thoroughly.
2. Heat the oil in a heavy-based saucepan, preferably non-stick, over a medium heat. Add the cummin seeds. As soon as the seeds begin to crackle, add the garlic and allow it to brown lightly.
3. Add the rice. Stir and fry for 2-3 minutes.
4. Add the salt and water. Stir and bring to the boil. Cover the pan tightly, reduce the heat to low and cook for 10 minutes. Do not lift the lid while the rice is cooking; this will result in loss of steam, which is vital in cooking rice successfully.
5. Remove the pan from the heat and leave it undisturbed for 8-10 minutes. Freshly cooked rice is very fragile, so please resist the temptation to stir and serve it straight away! Cooked rice will keep hot for up to 45 minutes if kept covered in the pot in which it is cooked.
6. Fork through the rice and transfer to a serving dish. Serve garnished with the coriander.

Serve with any meat, fish or chicken curry.

Suitable for freezing.

SIDE DISHES
AND PICKLES

Dhali Ambat
SERVES 4

This is a simple lentil and spinach dish with a superb flavour. The secret of success here is frying the red chillies and the fenugreek seeds to perfection. The souring agent used is Tamarind which is available in concentrated ready-to-use form from Indian grocers. If you cannot get it use lime juice, but the flavour will be different.

150g (5 oz) Masoor Dhal
(red split lentils), washed,
soaked in cold water for 30
minutes and drained
600ml (1 pint) water
3 tablespoons sunflower oil
1-2 long slim dried red chillies,
coarsely chopped
$^1/_2$ teaspoon fenugreek seeds
250g (8 oz) fresh spinach,
chopped (Frozen spinach may
be used, but use the leaf
spinach not purée.)
1 teaspoon ground turmeric
$1^1/_4$ teaspoons salt or to taste
90g (3 oz) coconut milk
powder
90ml (3 fl oz) hot water
$^1/_2$ teaspoon tamarind
concentrate or $1^1/_2$
tablespoons lime juice
1 small onion, approx. 125g
(4 oz), finely chopped

Preparation time: 20-25 minutes plus soaking
Cooking time: 45-50 minutes

1. Put the drained lentils and the water in a saucepan over a high heat and bring to the boil. Boil steadily without a lid for 10 minutes, then cover and simmer for 25-30 minutes or until the lentils are tender.
2. Meanwhile, heat 1 tablespoon of oil over a low heat and fry the dried chillies and fenugreek seeds gently, until they are just a shade darker. Stir constantly. Remove from the heat and cool in the pan. Crush them to a fine paste with the oil, using a pestle and mortar.
3. When the lentils are tender, add the spinach, turmeric and salt. Cover and simmer for 10 minutes.
4. Blend the coconut milk powder with the hot water and add to the lentils.
5. Add the crushed spice paste and tamarind. Stir and mix well and simmer for 5 minutes. Remove from the heat. If using lime juice, add this at the very end of the cooking.
6. In a separate pan, heat the remaining oil over a medium heat and fry the onions for 6-7 minutes or until pale golden. Stir frequently. Stir this into the lentils and serve.

Serve with Garlic Rice, Pork Assada and Brinjal Pickle.

Suitable for freezing only if fresh spinach is used.

Previous pages: Batata Ghashi and Dali Ambat.

Batata (Potato) Ghashi
SERVES 4

This potato dish is simplicity itself! It is quick to make and keeps extremely well for several days in the fridge. A tangy flavour is achieved by adding tamarind, which is an excellent natural preservative.

500g (1 lb) old potatoes, any
   variety except the floury ones
2 tablespoons sunflower oil
3 teaspoons ground coriander
1 teaspoon ground turmeric
$^1/_2$ teaspoon chilli powder
560ml (18 fl oz) warm water
1 teaspoon salt or to taste
60g (2 oz) coconut milk
   powder
90ml (3 fl oz) hot water
$^1/_4$ teaspoon tamarind
   concentrate or 1 tablespoon
   lime juice
2 heaped teaspoons ghee or
   unsalted butter
8 cloves of garlic, peeled and
   crushed

Preparation time: 15-20 minutes
Cooking time: 20 minutes

1. Peel and cut the potatoes into 2.5cm (1 inch) cubes.
2. Heat the oil over a low heat and add the ground coriander, turmeric and chilli powder. Fry for 1 minute.
3. Add the potatoes, water and salt. Bring to the boil, cover and boil for 10-12 minutes or until the potatoes are tender.
4. Blend the coconut milk powder with hot water and add to the drained potatoes.
5. Add the tamarind and stir until dissolved. If using lime juice, add this at the very end of cooking.
6. In a small pan heat the ghee or butter over a medium heat. Add the garlic and fry until lightly browned. Stir into the potatoes and remove from the heat and serve.

Serve with Chapatties accompanied by Meat Chilli Fry, Chicken Pot Roast etc.

Unsuitable for freezing.

Aubergine Curry
SERVES 4

*A*uberg*ine is known as 'Brinjal' in Goa and the rest of India. It is a very popular vegetable. Here the aubergines are simmered in a rich sauce using pre-roasted and ground poppy seeds, desiccated coconut and sesame seeds.*

1 medium aubergine, approx. 300g (10 oz)
300g (10 oz) peeled potatoes
1 tablespoon white poppy seeds
1 tablespoon sesame seeds
30g (1 oz) desiccated coconut
3 tablespoons sunflower oil
$^1/_4$ teaspoon fenugreek seeds
10-12 curry leaves, optional
1 large onion, approx. 250g (8 oz), finely sliced
2 teaspoons grated or minced fresh root ginger
2 teaspoons minced or crushed garlic
1 teaspoon ground cummin
1 teaspoon ground coriander
$^1/_2$ teaspoon ground turmeric
$^1/_2$-1 teaspoon chilli powder
1 teaspoon sweet paprika
560ml (18 fl oz) warm water
$1^1/_4$ teaspoons salt or to taste
1 tablespoon cider vinegar
90g (3 oz) chopped canned tomatoes with their juice

Preparation time: 30 minutes
Cooking time: 20 minutes

1. Cut the aubergine into 5cm (2 inch) cubes and soak in salted water for 30 minutes, then drain and rinse well under cold water.
2. Boil the potatoes until tender. Drain, cool, and cut into 5cm(2 inch) cubes.
3. Preheat a heavy-based frying pan over a medium heat and add the poppy and sesame seeds. Reduce the heat to low and dry roast the seeds until they just begin to brown. Add the coconut. Stir and roast the ingredients until they are light brown in colour. Put the ingredients on a plate and allow to cool. When cold, grind in batches in a coffee grinder until very fine.
4. Heat the oil over a medium heat and add the fenugreek seeds, curry leaves (if used)and the onions. Fry until the onions are soft, but not brown, about 5-6 minutes.
5. Add the ginger, garlic, cummin and coriander. Stir and fry for 1 minute. Add the ground ingredients and fry for 30 seconds. Add the turmeric, chilli powder and paprika. Stir and cook for 30 seconds.
6. Add the water and aubergines. Bring to the boil. Cover and cook over a medium heat for 10 minutes.
7. Add the potatoes, salt, vinegar and tomatoes. Cover and simmer for 2-5 minutes. Remove from the heat and serve.

Serve with Garlic Rice and Marinated Pork Chops.

Unsuitable for freezing.

Aubergine Curry.

Mung Bean Usal

SERVES 4

Mung beans are available in most good supermarkets and health food stores. If you can take the trouble to sprout the beans, they are an excellent source of vitamin C, and they look wonderful. Simply wash the beans and put them in a large glass bowl. Add lukewarm water to cover the beans, then cover the bowl with a plate. Leave in a warm place for 36-48 hours to sprout. Rinse the beans with lukewarm water and add fresh lukewarm water once or twice during sprouting. Drain and rinse before cooking.

250g (8 oz) mung beans, washed and soaked overnight, sprouted if wished
300ml (½ pint) water
2 tablespoons sunflower oil
1 teaspoon black mustard seeds
1 teaspoon cummin seeds
8-10 curry leaves, optional
1 large onion, approx. 250g (8 oz), finely chopped
1-2 fresh green chillies, seeded and sliced lengthwise
3.5cm (1½ inch) cube of fresh root ginger, peeled and cut into julienne sticks
1 teaspoon ground turmeric
½ teaspoon salt
½ teaspoon sugar
1 tablespoon lime juice

Preparation time: 10 minutes plus soaking
Cooking time: 15 minutes

1. Drain the mung beans and put into a saucepan with the water. Bring to the boil and cook over a medium heat, uncovered, for 10 minutes or until the beans are tender and they have absorbed most of the water. About 2 tablespoons of water should be left in the pan.
2. Heat the oil over a medium heat and add the mustard seeds. As soon as they pop, add the cummin seeds followed by the curry leaves, if used.
3. Add the onions, green chillies and ginger julienne and fry until the onions are soft, about 6-8 minutes.
4. Add the turmeric and fry for 30 seconds.
5. Add the mung beans, salt and sugar. Stir and mix well and cook for 2-3 minutes.
6. Stir in the lime juice and remove from the heat and serve.

Serve with Chapatties and Mutton Curry.

Batata Sukkhe
(Dry Spiced Potatoes)
SERVES 4

The humble potato is elevated to a gourmet status in this recipe! The coconut, which is roasted before being ground, is the key ingredient in enhancing the overall flavour.

60g (2 oz) desiccated coconut
500g (1 lb) old potatoes,
choose waxy and not the
    floury type
560ml (18 fl oz) water
1 teaspoon salt or to taste
¼ teaspoon tamarind
    concentrate or 1 tablespoon
    lime juice
2 tablespoons coconut oil or
    vegetable or corn oil
1 large onion, approx. 250g
    (8 oz), finely chopped
1 tablespoon ground coriander
¼ teaspoon ground cloves
¼ teaspoon freshly milled black
    pepper
½ teaspoon chilli powder
½ teaspoon ground turmeric
1 teaspoon sweet paprika

Preparation time: 15-20 minutes
Cooking time: 20-25 minutes

1. Preheat a heavy-based frying pan over a medium heat. Add the coconut and reduce the heat to low. Stir and dry roast for 1-2 minutes until lightly browned. Spread the coconut out on a large plate and allow to cool. When cold, grind in batches in a coffee grinder until fine.
2. Peel and cut the potatoes into 2.5cm (1 inch) cubes and put into a saucepan with the water. Bring to the boil. Cover and boil for 10-12 minutes or until the potatoes are tender.
3. Add the salt, tamarind and coconut. Stir and mix thoroughly and remove from the heat. If using lime juice, add this at the very end of cooking.
4. In a separate pan heat the oil over a medium heat and fry the onions for 6-7 minutes until they are a pale golden colour.
5. Add the ground coriander and fry for 30 seconds. Add the cloves and pepper. Stir and cook for 30 seconds. Add the chilli powder, turmeric and paprika. Stir and cook for 30 seconds.
6. Add this mixture to the potatoes and return the pan to the heat. Cook over a medium heat for 2-3 minutes. If using lime juice, add now and remove from the heat and serve.

Serve with Chapatties and Fried Chilli Chicken.

Unsuitable for freezing.

Cauliflower Ambat

SERVES 4

This is my mother-in-law's speciality and is a hot favourite in my family. Cauliflower is cooked in a light coconut-based sauce flavoured with fenugreek and chillies. The result is a dish with a subtle flavour and an enticing aroma!

2 teaspoons sunflower oil
¹/₂ teaspoon fenugreek seeds
1-2 long slim dried red chillies, chopped
90g (3 oz) unroasted shelled cashews, split
90g (3 oz) whole green beans, cut into 2.5cm (1 inch) pieces
450ml (15 fl oz) water
1 medium cauliflower, approx. 350g (12 oz), when outer leaves removed, cut into 1cm (¹/₂ inch) florets
1 teaspoon salt or to taste
45g (1¹/₂ oz) ghee or unsalted butter
1 medium onion, approx. 180g (6 oz), finely chopped
1 teaspoon ground turmeric
45g (1¹/₂ oz) coconut milk powder
180ml (6 fl oz) hot water
¹/₂ teaspoon tamarind concentrate or 1 tablespoon lime juice

Preparation time: 20-25 minutes
Cooking time: 15-20 minutes

1. Heat the oil in a small saucepan over a low heat and fry the fenugreek and chilli until they are just a shade darker. Remove from the heat and cool. Crush with a pestle and mortar, to make a paste using the oil in which they were fried.
2. Put the cashews and green beans in a saucepan with the water and bring to the boil. Reduce the heat, cover and cook for 5 minutes.
3. Add the cauliflower and salt. Cover and cook for a further 5 minutes. Add the crushed spice paste and stir well. Remove from the heat.
4. In a separate pan, heat the ghee or butter over a medium heat and fry the onions until they are a pale golden colour, about 6-7 minutes. Stir in the turmeric and fry for 1 minute. Stir this into the vegetables along with all the ghee or butter.
5. Blend the coconut milk powder with the hot water and add to the vegetables. Return to the heat and bring to a gentle simmer.
6. Add the tamarind and stir gently until dissolved. Cook gently without a lid for 5-6 minutes. If using lime juice, add now and remove from the heat and serve.

Serve with Beef Curry or Mutton Curry and plain boiled rice.

Suitable for freezing.

Cauliflower Ambat

Masala Dhal
SERVES 4

*D*hal is an important part of an Indian meal, especially for the vast majority of the vegetarian population. An amazing range of recipes based on pulses has been created by the 'Saraswat' community of Hindus. They originally lived in Goa though much of this small community has now moved to the district of Karnataka.

180g (6 oz) Masoor Dhal (red split lentils)

45g (1½ oz) ghee or unsalted butter

1 large onion, approx. 250g (8 oz), finely sliced

6-8 curry leaves, optional

4 cloves of garlic, peeled and crushed

Grind the following 5 ingredients in a coffee grinder until fine:

1-2 dried red chillies, chopped

2 teaspoons cummin seeds

2 teaspoons coriander seeds

1 teaspoons black peppercorns

4 whole cloves

30g (1 oz) desiccated coconut, ground in a coffee grinder until fine

1¼ teaspoons salt or to taste

1 teaspoon ground turmeric

785ml (25 fl oz) warm water

1 teaspoon tamarind concentrate or 1½ tablespoons lemon juice

2 tablespoons chopped fresh coriander leaves

Preparation time: 15 minutes plus soaking time
Cooking time: 40-45 minutes

1. Wash the lentils and soak in cold water for 1-2 hours, then drain well.

2. Melt the ghee or butter over a medium heat in a heavy-based saucepan and add the onions and curry leaves (if used). Fry the onions until they are soft, about 5-6 minutes.

3. Add the garlic and fry until the onions begin to brown. Stir frequently to ensure even cooking.

4. Adjust the heat to low and add the ground spices and coconut. Stir and fry for 2-3 minutes.

5. Add the dhal. Stir and fry over a medium heat for 2-3 minutes.

6. Add the salt and turmeric and cook for 1 minute.

7. Add the water and bring to the boil. Cover the pan and simmer for 30 minutes or until the lentils are tender and the mixture is thick.

8. Add the tamarind and stir until it is fully dissolved. If using lemon juice, simply stir it in.

9. Stir in the coriander leaves and remove from the heat and serve.

Serve with any meat, fish or seafood dishes accompanied by rice and/or bread.

Suitable for freezing.

Ford
(Goan Vegetables with Coconut)
SERVES 4

*T*his wonderful vegetable dish can be made with any easily available vegetables.
I have used two, cabbage and carrots, which most of us usually put into our
shopping trolley.

30g (1 oz) desiccated coconut
3 tablespoons sunflower oil
1¹/₂ teaspoons coriander seeds
¹/₄ teaspoon fenugreek seeds
1-2 dried red chillies, chopped
¹/₄ teaspoon black mustard
    seeds
8-10 curry leaves, optional
1 small onion, approx. 125g
    (4 oz), finely chopped
¹/₂ teaspoon ground turmeric
325g (11 oz) firm green
    cabbage, finely chopped
150g (5 oz) carrots, scraped
    and coarsely grated
1 teaspoon salt or to taste
1 teaspoon soft brown sugar
150ml (5 fl oz) warm water
¹/₄ teaspoon tamarind
    concentrate

Preparation time: 25 minutes
Cooking time: 15 minutes

1. Preheat a small heavy-based saucepan or frying
pan over a medium heat. Add the coconut and
reduce the heat to low. Stir and roast until coconut
is lightly browned, about 1-2 minutes. Transfer the
coconut to a plate and cool thoroughly.
2. Return the pan to the heat and add 1 tablespoon of oil. Add the coriander, fenugreek and red
chillies. Fry gently until the spices are a shade
darker, but do not brown. Remove from the heat
and cool.
3. Grind the roasted coconut and spices in a coffee
grinder until fine and set aside.
4. Heat the remaining oil over a medium heat and
add the mustard seeds and curry leaves, if used. As
soon as the seeds pop, add the onions and fry until
soft, but not brown.
5. Add the turmeric, cabbage, carrots, salt and
sugar. Stir and cook for 1-2 minutes.
6. Add the water and tamarind. Stir the tamarind
around in the water until dissolved. Stir and mix
well. Cover and simmer for 5 minutes.
7. Add the ground coconut mixture and stir until
the coconut has absorbed any cooking liquid left in
the pan. Remove from the heat and serve.

Serve as an accompaniment to any meat, fish or
seafood dish.

Suitable for freezing.

Vegetable Stew
SERVES 4

In the Portuguese/Indian mix of Goan cuisine, the strongest local influence is that of the Saraswat community, whose style of cooking is quite unique. This recipe is a classic example of their fabulous range.

1 medium cauliflower, 400g (14 oz) without leaves

180g (6 oz) potatoes, peeled

180g (6 oz) whole fresh green beans

60g (2 oz) ghee or unsalted butter

6 whole cloves

6 green cardamoms, split at the top of each pod

5cm (2 inch) piece cassia bark or cinnamon stick, halved

1 large red onion approx. 250g (8 oz), finely sliced

2-4 fresh green chillies, seeded and chopped

4 cloves of garlic, peeled and crushed

Grind the following 3 ingredients in a coffee grinder:

1 tablespoon white poppy seeds

1 tablespoon unroasted shelled cashews, lightly crushed

60g (2 oz) desiccated coconut

375ml (12 fl oz) warm water

1 teaspoon salt or to taste

1 level teaspoon tamarind concentrate or 1$^{1}/_{2}$ table-spoons lime juice

Preparation time: 25-30 minutes
Cooking time: 20 minutes

1. Cut the cauliflower into 2.5cm (1 inch) florets.
2. Boil the potatoes until just tender. Drain, cool, and dice.
3. Cut the beans in half and boil or steam until just tender.
4. Heat the ghee or butter over a medium heat and add the cloves, cardamoms and cassia or cinnamon. Cook for 30 seconds.
5. Add the onions and green chillies and fry until they are soft, but not brown, about 5-6 minutes. Stir frequently. Add the garlic and stir and fry for 1 minute. Add the ground ingredients. Fry over a low heat for 2 minutes, stirring constantly.
6. Add the water, salt and cauliflower. Bring to the boil, cover and simmer for 3-4 minutes. Add the cooked potatoes and beans. Simmer, uncovered, for 5 minutes.
7. Dissolve the tamarind in 3 tablespoons boiling water. Stir and add to the vegetables and mix thoroughly. If using lime juice, simply stir this in and remove from the heat and serve.

Serve with Jhinga Caldeen, Chicken Cafreal, Mashli Ghashi etc.

Unsuitable for freezing.

Vegetable Stew.

Broccoli Upkari
SERVES 4

India has 14 main languages and over a hundred dialects. The word 'Upkari' is believed to be derived from two words belonging to a South Indian language called 'Kannada'. 'Upu' means salt and 'kari' is chilli. Plenty of salt and chillies are used in the traditional 'Upkari' both of which I have used moderately in this recipe. You can use green cabbage or cauliflower instead of broccoli in this recipe.

3 tablespoons sunflower oil
$^{1}/_{2}$ teaspoon cummin seeds
3-4 cloves garlic, peeled and
   crushed
1-2 fresh green chillies, seeded
   and finely chopped
1 small onion, approx. 125g
   (4 oz), finely sliced
250g (8 oz) broccoli, cut into
   5 x 1cm (2 x $^{1}/_{2}$ inch) stems
$^{1}/_{2}$ teaspoon salt or to taste

Preparation time: 10-15 minutes
Cooking time: 15 minutes

1. Heat the oil over a medium heat and add the cummin. Immediately add the garlic and green chillies. Allow the garlic to brown lightly.
2. Add the onions and fry until they are soft, about 5-6 minutes. Stir frequently.
3. Add the broccoli and salt. Cover the pan tightly and reduce the heat to low. Sweat the broccoli for 8-10 minutes or until tender, but still firm.

Serve with any meat, fish or chicken dish.

Suitable for freezing.

Cucumber Raita
SERVES 4

Chopped cucumber in a delicately flavoured yogurt dressing will complement any spicy meal. The best type of yogurt for a Raita is one that is thick set and made with whole milk.

1 teaspoon cummin seeds
150g (5 oz) thick set natural
 yogurt
1 small clove of garlic, peeled
 and crushed
1/2 fresh green chilli, seeded and
 minced
1/2 teaspoon sugar
200g (7 oz) cucumber, finely
 chopped
45g (1 1/2 oz) salted roasted
 peanuts, lightly crushed
1/4 teaspoon salt or to taste

Preparation time: 15 minutes
Cooking time: Nil

1. Preheat a small heavy-based saucepan over a medium heat. When hot, add the cummin seeds and reduce the heat to low. Dry roast the seeds until they begin to release their aroma about 1-2 minutes. Remove and allow to cool. Crush them with a pestle and mortar or the back of a wooden spoon.
2. Put the yogurt in a bowl and beat until smooth.
3. Add the garlic, chilli, sugar and half the crushed cummin seeds. Mix well.
4. Add the cucumber, cover the bowl and chill until required.
5. Just before serving, add the peanuts and salt. Mix thoroughly and put Raita in a serving dish. Sprinkle the remaining cummin on top.

Serve with any meat, fish, seafood or vegetable dish.

Unsuitable for freezing.

Prawn Balchao
MAKES ABOUT 350-500G (12 OZ - 1 LB)

A well-known prawn pickle which will last well if you make sure the prawns are very well drained. Absence of moisture is the secret of its success, as with any pickle. Asaphoetida (hing) is an essential ingredient in this recipe and you can get it from Asian grocers in block or ground form. It should be used only in the specified quantity as it has a strong flavour.

1½ teaspoons salt
400g (14 oz) fresh cooked peeled small prawns or shrimps, frozen prawns should be thawed and drained first
125ml (4 fl oz) vegetable oil
½ teaspoon black mustard seeds
large pinch of asaphoetida (hing)
2 teaspoons ground turmeric
10 cloves of garlic, peeled and minced
2.5cm (1 inch) cube of fresh root ginger, peeled and finely grated
1-2 teaspoons chilli powder
2 teaspoons ground cummin
125ml (4 fl oz) cider vinegar

Preparation time: 10-15 minutes plus draining prawns
Cooking time: 10-15 minutes

1. Add 1 teaspoon of the salt to the prawns and tie up in a muslin cloth. Place in a colander over a bowl. Put a weight on top of the prawns and leave to drain for 1 hour.
2. Heat the oil over a medium heat. When the oil is almost smoking, add the mustard seeds and quickly follow with the asaphoetida (hing) and turmeric.
3. Add the prawns and fry for 5 minutes.
4. Add the garlic, ginger, remaining salt, chilli powder and cummin. Fry until all the moisture evaporates and oil begins to float on the surface.
5. Add the vinegar and remove from the heat.
6. Cool thoroughly and store in a moisture-free airtight jar in a cool dry place. This will keep for about 6 months.

The perfect partner for any pickle is dhal (lentils) and rice. You can, of course, serve any meat, fish or chicken dish of your choice. This pickle is also excellent with Chapatties.

Prawn Balchao, Lime Pickle and Carrot Raita

Lime Pickle

*L*ime Pickle is one of the best known Indian relishes. In India, pickles are eaten with rice and bread accompanied by various other dishes. I have been amused by watching Westerners pile up Lime Pickle on pappodums and munching away in Indian restaurants. I have tried it and am hooked on it! Make sure the limes are ripe for this recipe. They should not be dark green but rather a pale yellow colour. The dark green limes are too acidic and will make the pickle bitter.

750g (1½ lb) limes,
   about 10-11
1 tablespoon salt
125ml (4 fl oz) malt vinegar
250ml (8 fl oz) vegetable oil
1 teaspoon ground asaphoetida
   (hing)
10-12 cloves garlic, approx.
   30g (1 oz), peeled and
   crushed
15g (½ oz) piece of fresh root
   ginger, peeled and grated or
   minced
10-12 curry leaves, optional
Grind the following 3
ingredients together in a coffee
grinder:
2 tablespoons mustard seeds
1 tablespoon cummin seeds
2 teaspoons fenugreek seeds

2 teaspoons ground turmeric
2 teaspoons chilli powder
10 long slim whole fresh green
   chillies, halved
10 long slim whole fresh red
   chillies, halved
4 teaspoons salt
4 tablespoons sugar

Preparation time: 20 minutes plus 2 hours for draining
Cooking time: 35 minutes

1. Wash the limes and dry thoroughly with a cloth. Top and tail them and cut them into quarters.
2. Sprinkle with the salt and put the salted limes in a colander. Set aside for 2 hours over a bowl.
3. Transfer the limes to a large bowl and add the vinegar. Stir until any remaining salt is dissolved, then drain again.
4. Heat the oil in a saucepan over a medium heat and add the asaphoetida (hing). Immediately follow with the garlic, ginger and curry leaves if used. Allow the garlic and ginger to brown slightly.
5. Add the ground ingredients, turmeric and chilli powder. Stir and fry for 1 minute.
6. Add the fresh chillies, salt and sugar. Cook for 1 minute and add the limes. Remove from heat and cool completely.
7. Store in sterilised airtight jars. Allow 4-5 weeks to mature. This will keep for 8-10 months.

Carrot Raita
SERVES 4

250g (8 oz) carrots, peeled and
   cut into 5mm (^{1}/$_4$ inch) cubes
30g (1 oz) desiccated coconut,
   ground until fine
1 fresh green chilli, seeded and
   chopped
100ml (3^1/$_2$ fl oz) hot water
150g (5 fl oz) thick natural
   yogurt
^{1}/$_2$ teaspoon salt
2 teaspoons sunflower oil
^{1}/$_2$ teaspoon black mustard
   seeds
^{1}/$_2$ teaspoon cummin seeds

Preparation time: 5-10 minutes
Cooking time: 5 minutes

1. Steam the carrots until just tender. Allow to cool thoroughly.
2. Soak the coconut and chilli in hot water. Cover and set aside for 10-15 minutes.
3. Put the yogurt in a bowl and beat until smooth. Add the salt, carrots and coconut/chilli mixture.
4. Heat the oil in a small saucepan over a medium heat. Add the mustard seeds and as soon as they pop, add the cummin. Allow the seeds to crackle then pour hot oil seasoning over the Raita. Stir and mix well. Chill before serving.

Brinjal (Aubergine) Pickle
MAKES ABOUT 350-500G (12 OZ - 1 LB)

1 aubergine, approx.400g
   (14 oz) peeled and diced
1 tablespoon salt
125ml (4 fl oz) vegetable oil
^{1}/$_2$ teaspoon ground
   asaphoetida (hing)
10 cloves garlic, approx.
   30g (1 oz) peeled and crushed
5cm (2 inch) cube fresh root
   ginger, peeled and grated
1 teaspoon mustard seeds
1 teaspoon fenugreek seeds
1^1/$_2$ teaspoons cummin seeds
30g (1 oz) sugar
20g (^{3}/$_4$ oz) salt
180ml (6 fl oz) white wine
   vinegar

Preparation time: 20 minutes plus draining
Cooking time: 25-30 minutes

1. Sprinkle the aubergine with salt and mix well. Tie up in a muslin cloth. Place in a colander over a bowl and put a weight on top to drain off the water. This will take 6-7 hours.
2. Heat the oil over a medium heat and lightly brown the asaphoetida (hing) and crushed garlic. Reduce the heat and add ginger and fry for 1 minute. Grind the mustard, fenugreek, and cummin seeds. Add to the pan, and fry for 2 minutes.
3. Add the sugar, salt, aubergines and vinegar. Simmer gently for 20-25 minutes or until tender.
4. Cool thoroughly and store in a sterilised air-tight jar. Allow 10-12 days to mature.

SWEETS AND DESSERTS

Sabu Dane Che Alone
SERVES 4-6

Sago cooked in fresh coconut milk with nuts and raisins is an unusual and delicious taste. Fresh coconut milk is rather laborious to prepare, so I succumb to the instant creamed coconut which is sold in most supermarkets! You could also use canned coconut milk if you wish, but you may need to increase the quantity.

125g (4 oz) sago or tapioca
300ml (1/2 pint) fresh milk
125ml (4 fl oz) hot water
60g (2 oz) creamed coconut,
  cut into small pieces
90g (3 oz) caster sugar
1/4 teaspoon salt
1 teaspoon ground cardamom
1/4 teaspoon ground cinnamon
1/4 teaspoon ground nutmeg
30g (1 oz) unsalted butter
30g (1 oz) sultanas
45g (1 1/2 oz) unroasted shelled
  cashews, lightly crushed with
  a rolling pin

Preparation time: 15 minutes
Cooking time: 20-25 minutes

1. Rinse the sago or tapioca in cold water. Drain thoroughly and set aside.
2. Put the milk, hot water, coconut, sugar and salt into a heavy-based saucepan. Bring to a gentle simmer and cook until the coconut has dissolved.
3. Add the sago or tapioca and cook over a medium heat until the mixture is thick. The sago will stick to the bottom and sides of the pan during cooking. When it thickens, it will stop sticking, leaving the saucepan base and sides clean. When you reach this stage, which will take 10-12 minutes, remove the pan from the heat.
4. Add the cardamom, cinnamon and nutmeg. Stir and mix thoroughly.
5. In a separate pan, melt the butter gently and add the sultanas. When they start sizzling, add the cashews and fry until the cashews are lightly browned.
6. Remove half the sultanas and cashews with a slotted spoon and set aside. Add the remainder, along with all the butter, to the sago or tapioca and mix well.
7. Put the mixture into a decorative 600ml (1 pint) mould and allow to cool for an hour, then turn out onto a serving dish. Spoon the remaining sultanas and cashews around the base and serve at room temperature.

Unsuitable for freezing.

Previous pages: Neuris and Small Coconut Cakes.

Neuris
(Sweet Samosas)
MAKES 12

*N*euri is a traditional dish cooked during the Hindu festival of "Diwali" (festival of lights) and it is a Christmas speciality for the Christians.

75g (2¹/₂ oz) desiccated coconut

45g (1¹/₂ oz) light soft brown sugar

30g (1 oz) unroasted shelled cashews, lightly crushed with a rolling pin

30g (1 oz) seedless raisins

250ml (8 fl oz) evaporated milk

¹/₂ teaspoon ground nutmeg

¹/₂ teaspoon ground cinnamon

12 sheets of filo pastry, approx. 28 x 18cm (11 x 7 inch)

sunflower oil or melted butter to brush over the pastry

Preparation time: 20 minutes

Cooking time: 30-35 minutes

1. Put the coconut, sugar, cashews, raisins and evaporated milk into a small, heavy-based saucepan and place over a medium heat.

2. Stir and mix the ingredients thoroughly and as soon as the milk starts bubbling, reduce the heat to low. Cook, uncovered, until the coconut has absorbed all the milk, about 8-10 minutes. Stir frequently.

3. Remove the pan from the heat and stir in the nutmeg and cinnamon. Allow to become cold. Divide into 12 equal portions.

4. Preheat the oven to 180°C, 350°F, Gas Mark 4.

5. Line a baking sheet with greased greaseproof paper or non-stick baking parchment.

6. Place a sheet of filo pastry on a pastry board and brush well with oil or butter. Fold the pastry in half lengthwise. Brush with oil or butter again and fold it widthwise.

7. Place a portion of filling on one half of the pastry and fold the other half over it. Seal the edges with cold water. Press the edges with a fork and trim with a pair of scissors.

8. Place the Samosas on the prepared baking sheet and brush liberally with oil or melted butter.

9. Bake in the centre of the oven for 20-25 minutes or until the Samosas are golden brown.

Serve with morning coffee or afternoon tea.

Suitable for freezing.

Bibinca
SERVES 4-6

This is a traditional coconut cake which is made by stacking together thin layers of pancakes. It is a Christmas speciality and is very rich and delicious!

125g (4 oz) plain flour
½ teaspoon ground nutmeg
½ teaspoon ground cinnamon
6 medium egg yolks
150g (5 oz) caster sugar
180g (6 oz) creamed coconut,
   cut into small pieces and
   dissolved in 375ml (12 fl oz)
   boiling water and cooled
60g (2 oz) ghee, melted

Preparation time: 15-20 minutes
Cooking time: 55-60 minutes

1. Mix the flour, nutmeg and cinnamon together.
2. Put the egg yolks in a large bowl and add the sugar. Beat until the mixture is light and creamy. Stir in the flour mixture.
3. Gradually add the cold coconut milk and beat to a smooth batter. Cover and leave for 1 hour.
4. Preheat the grill to medium. Preheat the oven to 200°C, 400°F, Gas Mark 6.
5. Line a 23cm (9 inch) round cake tin with non-stick baking parchment.
6. Heat ½ tablespoon of melted ghee in a 20cm (8 inch) frying pan over a medium heat.
7. Spread 4 tablespoons batter over the base of the pan and allow to set, then turn off the heat. Place the pancake under the grill, and cook until browned. Remove and spread 2 teaspoons of melted ghee on the cooked side. Spread 4 table-spoons batter over this and return to the grill. Allow to brown and repeat with melted ghee and batter as before, until all the batter is used.
8. When the pancakes are ready, loosen the edges with a thin spatula and shake the pan to loosen the cake. Lift the cake out carefully and place in the prepared cake tin. Bake in the centre of the oven for 15 minutes or until well browned.
9. Allow to cool, then transfer to a serving dish. Cut into slices like a cake.

Serve as a dessert or with morning coffee.

Unsuitable for freezing.

Bibinca

Small Coconut Cakes
(Bolinho De Coco)
MAKES 16

*T*hese delicious little coconut cakes are absolutely gorgeous! Do try and get the finer cut of dessicated coconut which is sold in good supermarkets and, of course, Indian grocers.

180ml (6 fl oz) water
125g (4 oz) caster sugar
1 teaspoon ground cardamom
or any other flavouring such
as vanilla
180g (6 oz) fine desiccated
coconut
1 tablespoon sesame seeds
45g (1¹/₂ oz) unroasted shelled
cashews, lightly crushed with
a rolling pin
1 tablespoon plain flour
2 medium eggs, beaten until
light and fluffy
1 egg white, lightly beaten

Preparation time: 10 minutes plus cooling
Cooking time: 35 minutes

1. Put the water and sugar into a saucepan and bring to the boil over a high heat. Reduce the heat to medium and let it bubble for 5-6 minutes or until the syrup thickens slightly.
2. Add the ground cardamom or vanilla, then the coconut. Stir until the coconut has absorbed all the syrup. Remove from the heat and cool thoroughly.
3. Add the sesame seeds, cashews, flour and eggs and mix thoroughly.
4. Preheat the oven to 180°C, 350°F, Gas Mark 4.
5. Divide the mixture into 16 equal-sized portions and shape each into a smooth, flat, 1cm (¹/₂ inch) thick cake.
6. Line a baking sheet with greased greaseproof paper or non-stick baking parchment. Dip each cake in egg white and place on the baking sheet 3.5cm (1¹/₂ inch) apart. Bake in the centre of the oven for 25-30 minutes or until golden brown. Remove and cool on a wire rack.

Serve with after dinner coffee or morning/afternoon tea or coffee.

Suitable for freezing.

Mango Mousse
SERVES 4-6

The mango purée used in this recipe is made from "Alphonso" mango which is a canned purée, sold by Asian grocers. Brand names such as "Lotus" and "Fortune" are quite similar to Alphonso mango.

1 packet lemon flavoured jelly
90ml (3 fl oz) cold water
470g (15 fl oz) puréed mango
250ml (8 fl oz) double cream
75g (2¹/₂ oz) caster sugar
1 teaspoon ground cardamom
  or 1¹/₂ tablespoons rosewater
To decorate:
2 kiwi fruit, skinned and sliced
470g (15 oz) canned lychees,
  drained
250g (8 oz) canned guava
  halves, drained, pips removed
  and each half cut in two
250g (8 oz) canned sliced
  mangoes, drained

Preparation time: 10 minutes
Cooking time: None

1. Separate the cubes of jelly and place in a jug.
2. Add the cold water and microwave on HIGH for 1 minute. (Timing for a 650 watt oven.) Alternatively, dissolve the jelly in the conventional way.
3. Allow the jelly to cool slightly, then whisk until frothy.
4. Gradually add the mango purée whilst still whisking. Let the mixture stand for 30-35 minutes, then whisk again.
5. Whisk the cream until thick, but not stiff. Add to the mango mixture in batches. Whisk for 30 seconds between each addition.
6. Add the sugar and ground cardamom or rosewater. Whisk until well blended.
7. Rinse out a 23cm (9 inch) diameter ring tin in cold water and pour the mixture into it. Cover and leave to set in the refrigerator overnight. Alternatively, set the mousse in a glass bowl.
8. Rinse a serving dish in cold water and turn out the mousse. Fill the centre of the ring with lychees and arrange the rest of the fruits around the edge.
9. If the mousse is set in a bowl, serve decorated with chopped canned or fresh mangoes and a little whipped cream.

Unsuitable for freezing.

Banana Fritters
(Filoss)
SERVES 4

A *quick and simple dish to make, which is full of subtle flavours and varied textures. The batter is flavoured with nutmeg and cinnamon and the finished dish is glazed with apricot jam and brandy, then garnished with toasted almonds.*

150g (5 oz) plain flour
½ teaspoon ground nutmeg
1 teaspoon ground cinnamon
2 tablespoons granulated sugar
½ teaspoon salt
4 large ripe bananas, coarsely
  chopped
2 medium eggs
125ml (4 fl oz) milk
Oil for deep frying
1 tablespoon brandy, optional
1 heaped tablespoon apricot
  jam
1½ tablespoons toasted flaked
almonds

Preparation time: 10-15 minutes
Cooking time: 15 minutes

1. Put the flour in a mixing bowl and add the nutmeg, cinnamon, sugar and salt. Mix well, then add the bananas.
2. Beat the eggs and gradually add the milk whilst still beating. Add the egg mixture to the flour. Stir and mix until the batter coats the bananas fully.
3. Heat the oil in a deep fat frying pan over a medium heat. Heat to 160°C (325°F). Put in as many dessertspoon sized dollops of batter as the pan will hold easily without overcrowding. Fry the fritters until they are evenly browned on both sides. Drain on absorbent paper.
4. Arrange the fritters on a serving dish. Pour the brandy (if used) evenly over the fritters.
5. Heat the apricot jam until just beginning to bubble. Stir and brush evenly over the fritters.
6. Sprinkle the toasted almonds on top. Serve at room temperature.

Unsuitable for freezing.

Index